Bipolar In Order

Looking At Depression, Mania, Hallucination, And Delusion From The Other Side

Tom Wootton

with Peter Forster MD, Maureen Duffy PhD, Brian Weller, Scott Sullender PhD, Michael Edelstein PhD, and other contributors

Bipolar Advantage, Publishers
San Francisco

Bipolar In Order

www.BipolarInOrder.com

Internet addresses given in this book were accurate at the time the book went to press.

Cover design by Don Farnsworth
www.magnoliaeditions.com

ISBN 978-0-9774423-4-8

Practical yet profound, simple yet deep, in-the-moment yet timeless, **Bipolar in Order** *provides a view of this condition that does not shy away from its devastating consequences but that does promote acceptance, insight, responsibility, and-ultimately-mastery. Although Wootton does romanticize serious mental illness, he and his collaborators provide the essential message that symptom reduction or elimination is far from the main goal of adaptation and intervention. Sure to challenge traditional thinking, this important book is integrative and wise.*

Stephen P. Hinshaw, PhD
Professor and Chair, Department of Psychology, UC Berkeley

As a person who has experienced the depths of despair associated with mental illness, Tom's premise that our dark times can lead to a greater understandings of ourselves is a welcome message. Healing and recovery become possible when a person is surrounded by a support network. The second half of **Bipolar In Order** *is visionary as persons from different disciplines share the ideal of an integrated approach to support persons who journey with a mental illness. The reality is that it is already difficult to achieve health care parity for persons living with mental health issues much less put together an extensive support team. Tom's book sets forth the model that we should all be working for.*

Susan Gregg-Schroeder
Coordinator of Mental Health Ministries

With increasing frequency mental health professionals are acknowledging the positive benefits of mildly manic states, such as energy, drive and creativity, but Wootton takes that trend further than few shrinks would dare, declaring bipolar is not a disorder at all, in essence proclaiming for himself and his fellow bipolars: we are here and we are not a mistake. He offers a comprehensive program for bipolars to find their own type of balance--to be themselves and in control at the same time.

John D. Gartner, PhD
The Hypomanic Edge: The Link Between (a Little) Craziness and (a Lot) of Success in America

Tom Wootton knows that people with bipolar disorder can turn what they perceive as "negatives" into strengths and lead meaningful, productive lives. His philosophy focuses on success, rather than anticipation of failure. He has lived it in his personal and professional life, and he cares deeply about those who hear his message. This is an inspiring book that offers practical tools for living life to its fullest.

Liz T. Smith, Director
NAMI Center for Leadership Development

I admire your courage, and the way in which you are using your own experience of bipolarity to try to help others. Indeed, the main message -- which comes across very clearly -- is definitely needed: Bipolar disorder is not something to be ashamed of; it is not a "life sentence"; and with proper attention, it need not even be regarded as a disease.

Jim Phelps, MD
Why Am I Still Depressed? Recognizing and Managing the Ups and Downs of Bipolar II and Soft Bipolar Disorder

Tom Wootton has written an unusual book growing out of his own manic depressive illness. He explores the positive value of mania and depression, linking it to Eastern traditions of mental discipline, while at the same time appreciating the need for warranted medical diagnosis and treatment. He also describes a team approach oriented towards recovery rather than remission. While complex, and not one size fits all, his approach may help many better understand, treat, and appreciate this condition.

S. Nassir Ghaemi MD MPH
Professor of Psychiatry, Director, Mood DisordersProgram, Tufts Medical Center

Table of Contents

Acknowledgments

Special thanks to the Education Team, who not only created the workshop programs, but wrote elegantly about them and the *Advantage Program Components* chapters for this book: Peter Forster, MD, Maureen Duffy, PhD, Brian Weller, Scott Sullender, PhD, and Michael R. Edelstein, PhD.

The contributing authors deserve much recognition for joining the project. Their chapters make a tremendous difference and their perspectives add much to the book. Contributors include: Rochelle I. Frank, PhD; James W. Jordan, Jr.; Maria Chang-Calderon, PhD(c), MSHR; Denise K. Hughes, M.A.; Justin Liu, MD; Ruth Leyse-Wallace PhD, RD; Mark Jenkins; and Will Meecham, MD.

During the writing of the book, many people participated by contributing ideas and feedback at my talks and proofreading the book. Outstanding among them include: Bramachari Lee, Ellen Nadeau, Anthony Blackhorse, Phyllis Le Chat, David Calvert, Cathy Vaught, Heidi Alberti, and Karen Randolph.

This book is much better written than my previous efforts because of the quality of editing. I am sure my future work will show the lessons that they taught me in the process. Editors include Kate Grimsrud and Kareen Carter.

Preface

"Those who dance are considered insane by those who can't hear the music."

- George Carlin

When Christopher Columbus set sail for the new world, the common belief was that the world was flat and he would fall off. Once he saw the world from the other side and spoke of its many wonders, the world became a far more beautiful place.

Yet many people still clung to the old belief and could not accept the new evidence. It took many years for the world to adjust to the truth. To this day there are still some who believe the world is flat, but most of us consider them ignorant and unable to accept reality.

When I set out to explore the inner world, the common belief was that I would fall off the edge too. But just as Columbus discovered a world filled with beauty, I have seen depression, mania, hallucination, and delusion from the other side and found incredible vistas. With training, you too can visit those worlds without falling off, and discover a life far more beautiful than you can imagine.

What is unfortunate today is that far too many people continue to cling to the old belief that it is impossible to live a full life with a mental condition. On the other hand, a growing group of people are beginning to consider a life that is not restricted to a narrow range of experience. I look forward to the day when we all rise above the ignorance that keeps us in fear and denial of a better life.

Bipolar In Order is based on a very simple premise: we can learn and grow to the point that we see our condition as an advantage in our lives. Because this concept is often difficult for many people to accept on blind faith alone, I encourage everyone to simply begin by accepting that this new perspective is possible. To make this perspective a reality requires persistence, determination, and commitment. If you will give this perspective a chance, you will prove it in your own life.

There are so many examples of bipolar "disorder" that it is easy to understand why so many people try to avoid it instead of facing it and getting it under control. We can choose to view depression, mania, hallucination, and delusion from at least two different perspectives--either as "disorder" or as "in order." Knowing that we have a choice of perspectives leads us to the understanding that we do not have to accept a diminished life. We begin to see what bipolar can be if we get it "in order" instead of trying to make it go away.

For me, *Bipolar In Order* is the greatest state there is. Once you begin to see the new perspective, everything changes. You see why the current approach of avoidance is all wrong. You cannot get to *Bipolar In Order* by figuring out how to avoid the symptoms. Avoidance is accepting a diminished life tragically below that which is possible. This book is about what bipolar looks like from the perspective of "in order" and how you can achieve it in your own life.

My first two books detail some of the steps and show the early phases of my thinking that have led to this book. The brief descriptions below are to put this book in context.

The Bipolar Advantage is about more than simply accepting your condition and how difficult it can be; it is also about learning to employ the tools to create a better future. More than anything else, it is a marker for where my thinking was in 2005. Many of the concepts are just as valid today, but looking back on it from today's perspective, it shows what kind of growth in thinking and behavior is possible in a short amount of time.

The Depression Advantage is about rising above depression and realizing you have it within yourself to handle the condition. It was where my thinking was in 2007 and shows major changes in the two years since *The Bipolar Advantage* was written. While the concepts from the first book are still included (as they are in this book), depressive states were also addressed as I had begun to change my perception and ability to understand them. When I wrote *The Depression Advantage*, I still saw depression as a burden to overcome, but saw great benefits in "rising above the pain" and gaining from the lessons that are available from doing so.

In my talks, workshops, and personal experiences during 2008, I realized there was much more to explore. A huge breakthrough occurred during a keynote speech I was giving for San Bernardino County Mental Health Department. I realized I was experiencing the same symptoms of my deepest depression several years ago when I tried to kill myself, yet was now functioning at a very high level. I didn't develop this ability by "rising above the pain," I got there by seeing the pain as no different than any other state. This perspective is called "equanimity."

I began to realize that no state of mind is better or worse than any other. It is intensity of experience that really matters--realizing that we can live with equal intensity in all states. While in equanimity, we can appreciate any state for what it is without prejudging ourselves or the state as either bad or good. These states of equanimity are often called self-realization, ecstasy, or bliss.

Of course, the only way to prove we have attained equanimity is to change our behavior, which is what self-mastery is all about. We all have it within ourselves to master our thoughts and actions to become more saint-like in our relations with others.

Bipolar In Order is about defining success on our terms, developing the skills to achieve it, and doing the work necessary to turn it into a reality. The book is divided into four sections and a conclusion: *Results Worth Striving For, What Is In The Way, How To Get There,* and *Advantage Program Components;* concluding with *Where Do We Go From Here?.*

Results Worth Striving For sets the bar for what we are capable of. In spelling out real ways that our conditions can be advantageous in our lives, this section is the most challenging part of the book. We may not all desire to achieve such states as described in this section, but we must understand that our beliefs about what we can achieve create the limits of our success. Much better to believe we can achieve greatness and settle for a good life than to believe that even a good life is out of our reach.

What Is In The Way looks at the beliefs about mental illness that are holding us back. Pulling no punches, this section examines the wrong beliefs and practices that contribute to the tremendous suffering experienced by the majority of the people who have been diagnosed with a mental condition.

How To Get There lays out clear measurable steps we can use as a roadmap to success. The steps include building an integrated team, education, assessment, life planning, and treatment.

Advantage Program Components outlines the main components to assemble an integrated team. A representative from each discipline briefly describes their point of view, integration with the team, assessment process, goal setting for the Life Plan, and treatment regimen. By seeing all of the main components and how they relate to one another, you can use this section as a guide to building your own team.

It is important to point out Columbus had highly developed skills, worthy tools, and an able crew. He was well-trained to navigate to his destination and had the skills to handle the rough seas that he encountered on the way. It also helps that he may have been bipolar or at least hypomanic![1]

The path to *Results Worth Striving For* includes developing the skills, using the tools, and building a team to help you accomplish your goals. I look forward to joining you on a path to a better life.

---

1 Gartner, John D., The Hypomanic Edge, 2005, Simon & Schuster, N.Y., p.28

Results Worth Striving For

The mental health field is plagued with the bigotry of low expectations. Far too many people are talking about "changing the stigma," while creating the worst stigma of all--the idea that we are not capable of achieving greatness. While their intentions are good, they are doing terrible harm to everyone with a mental condition and those who love and support them. This "can't do" attitude is rampant in professionals, consumers, friends and family, and advocates. So attached are they to their self-defeating view, some even attack anyone who suggests that we can have a better life. It is time to stand up to such negativity by describing real *Results Worth Striving For*.

Every human being is capable of achieving greatness. We can make our lives meaningful if we set goals that challenge ourselves while making sure that they are not so difficult that we get discouraged. *Bipolar In Order* is about setting realistic goals with the help of your entire team and having the support to make them happen. Making them happen means setting achievable milestones and adjusting the steps as necessary along the way. Your personal "Life Plan" includes milestones as well as concrete actions to take on the first day. Once the first milestones are accomplished, you gain the confidence and skills to achieve your highest aspirations.

Depending on our starting point, habits, and resistance to change, we may begin with modest goals; but, we must also accept what is possible with enough time and effort. Anything else is accepting a diminished life.

A truly great life encompasses your entire life as a whole, not just parts of it. Your Life Plan needs to be all inclusive as well, and address all areas: Physical, Mental, Emotional, Spiritual, Relationships, and Career/Financial.

Our ultimate possibilities:

- Clear Insight
- True Freedom
- Real Stability
- Self-Mastery
- Equanimity
- Perspective

By spelling out clear *Results Worth Striving For*, I hope to inspire you to strive for the possibilities that are achievable by those who set their minds to it. Of course, we cannot achieve these results overnight. We must set reasonable goals in the short term while maintaining the possibility that the goals outlined in this section can eventually be attained. The process of setting goals and creating a path to success is covered in detail in the third section: *How To Get There*.

Clear Insight

"The old paradigm is for us to avoid emotional pain at all costs while remaining ignorant of the lessons that are available to us."
- The Depression Advantage[1]

The medical definition of "insight" reads, "understanding or awareness of one's mental or emotional condition; especially: recognition that one is mentally ill "[2] By that definition I have no insight because I don't recognize my condition as an illness.

Allow me to suggest that insight is the ability to recognize my condition and all of the aspects associated with it. It means not only recognizing the cause of the condition, but the whole experience. We all have some degree of insight or we would not be able to function. The degree of insight that we have determines the degree that we have our condition "in order." Insight is the foundation of *Bipolar In Order*.

If we learn to examine our condition, instead of just the causes of it, we can begin to gain clear awareness into what it is and how it affects our lives. With that insight comes understanding and the wisdom to choose how we react to our circumstances. Virginia Woolf said, "You can't find

---

1 Wootton, Tom, The Depression Advantage, 2007 Bipolar Advantage Publishers, CA

2 insight. (n.d.). Merriam-Webster's Medical Dictionary. Retrieved October 31, 2009, from Dictionary.com website: http://dictionary.reference.com/browse/insight

peace by avoiding life."[1] We must examine our lives if we are to gain the insight that leads to peace.

Wisdom comes from examining all of the aspects of our condition: physical, mental, emotional, and spiritual. We also need to examine how our condition affects our relationships and career/financial life. The more deeply we look into all of these aspects, the more subtle our perceptions become.

In *The Depression Advantage*[2] I wrote about my own examination of depression. Not only did I look closely at my own experiences, but also at the lives of Saints who transcended depression by acknowledging and learning from it. By doing so they changed the perspective in their own lives and the lives of everyone around them.

An example of how this applies to schizophrenia is the movie *A Beautiful Mind*, the story of John Nash.[3] John had a very strong ability to hallucinate and have delusions. In the beginning of the movie his hallucinations helped him to see solutions to mathematical problems. This ability earned him the Nobel Prize.

Unfortunately, John could not tell his hallucinations and delusions from "normal" reality due to his lack of awareness regarding his mental condition. His lack of insight into his condition almost killed him and those he loved. As he became more aware, he developed the ability to

---

1 Hare, David, The Hours, screenplay, 2002 Paramount Pictures and Miramax USA and Britain

2 Wootton, Tom, The Depression Advantage, 2007, Bipolar Advantage Publishers, CA, p. 21-30

3 Goldsman, Akiva, A Beautiful Mind, screenplay, 2001, Imagine Entertainment, USA

recognize the difference between "normal" experiences and his hallucinations and was able to live with them to some extent. Although limited in his abilities, John gained the ability to function and return to work.

Toward the end of the movie, John was leaving his classroom along with some students when a stranger came up to see him. He turned to one of his students and asked if that person was real. His student asked, "Why, do you still see people?" John replied, "Yes, but I choose to ignore them."[1] He clearly had developed enough insight to recognize the difference at least some of the time.

It is very clear to me from watching the movie and from seeing interviews of the real John Nash that he no longer possesses the ability to earn another Nobel Prize. But, what if he had been taught to not only recognize his hallucinations and delusions, but to see value in them? How many more Nobel Prizes might he have won if he had harnessed those abilities to his advantage instead of just gaining enough insight to ignore them?

We all have seen how some insight has led to a greater ability to both control and avoid states like depression. Nonetheless, many still believe the deeper states are too much for them to understand. They gain enough awareness to recognize that the deeper states are coming and take steps to avoid them, but end up living in fear, hoping that they can avoid the states forever. Deep down inside they

---

1 Howard, Ron, A Beautiful Mind, director and producer, 2001, Imagine Entertainment, USA

Note: In speaking about this with thousands of people, nobody has questioned the accuracy of the story and many recall the part of the movie just as I describe it. In watching the movie recently, I realized that it did not happen all in one scene, but was a combination of three separate scenes. It is interesting how the mind can be so easily triggered to recollect something that did not even happen. Did it happen to you too?

know that someday it might come back and they will have no skills to be able to face the condition.

Those of us who seek insight into the condition itself, rather than merely how to avoid it, find that we understand it so deeply that the condition loses its power over us. This awareness doesn't happen overnight, but the more we experience our condition with an approach toward gaining insight, the greater our ability to endure it without losing control. We find that we can function at deeper and deeper levels. With greater insight, we begin to recognize that deeper states are only a matter of degree. As our understanding grows, we find that much deeper states begin to fall within our ability to function just fine. We eventually get to the point that we can even see advantages in it.

This understanding reduces the risk of suicide because we are no longer out of control. It also leads to freedom, stability, and the other results outlined in this section.

Similar insights are available regarding every condition in our lives if we just look for them. Such insights are the difference between a diminished life and one of greatness. Once we accept that we have the capability of understanding even the deepest states, we are well on the way to becoming free to choose our reactions based on the wisdom that we have developed. If we do not develop the wisdom to choose our reactions, we will inevitably revert to the old patterns of avoidance and fear.

True Freedom

"I want freedom for the full expression of my personality."
- *Mahatma Gandhi*

Everybody wants to be free. Freedom is touted as the most basic of human rights. The commonly understood definitions of freedom are "the power or right to act, speak, or think as one wants without hindrance or restraint"[1] or "the power of self-determination attributed to the will; the quality of being independent of fate or necessity."[2] Yet, by the very definitions, none of us are truly free. We mistakenly limit freedom to a very narrow range of experience.

A child's view of freedom is to be free from the direction of parents, teachers, and other people of authority. Even when we become adults, we often cling to the same narrow definition: freedom from coercion of others. But there is a much greater freedom that most of us have never even considered: freedom to choose how to react to every stimulus.

Our power of self-determination is mostly at the whim of circumstances which we mistakenly believe we have no control over. Every stimulus that we encounter generates a response that is more often beyond our control than within the guidance of our wisdom.

---

1 New Oxford American Dictionary, 2nd Edition

2 Ibid

The stimulus/response mechanism is easy for us to understand at a basic level. When we put our hand on a hot stove and automatically pull away, the stimulus of extreme heat creates an automatic response that protects us from being burned. We can't imagine being able to leave our hand on the stove or even why anyone would want to. The stimulus of hunger drives us to eat, pain makes us pull away, and something we find attractive drives us to pursue it. For the most part, we have no choice but to react. We are usually not even aware that choice is possible.

Some stimulus/response mechanisms are clearly advantageous. Without these mechanisms we would end up injured or dead, but those are the minority of circumstances. Most cases are typically our habitual reactions to things like bumper stickers and other "triggers." We react the way we have trained ourselves to react, without thought or wisdom. Even while responding in the same old way, we know we could behave differently or produce a better outcome, but we react out of habit instead. We often react to the stimulus of our thoughts in ways that are harmful to ourselves and others. True freedom is to have the choice to react to all stimuli based on our insight and wisdom instead of automatic responses.

If you think that you are free to choose how to react, go without eating for a day. The stimulus of hunger will become your main focus. By the end of the day you will be unable to think of anything but food and will think you are going to die unless you eat right away. Although the stimulus of hunger is necessary and beneficial, it is completely false that you will die after such a short period of time. Most people can go for thirty-two days without food before they die.

Almost all of us can go a day or so with no serious repercussions. Some would even say that we are better off periodically going without food for a day or more.

Fasting is a spiritual practice shared by most religions. Fasting means purposely going without food for an extended period of time such as a day, a week, or longer. Those of us who practice fasting have insight into how the stimulus of hunger works. We rapidly get to the point where that stimulus of hunger no longer controls our lives. Besides the clear health benefits, its deeper purpose is to help us gain insight into all of our desires and gain wisdom that leads to true freedom in all circumstances.

When you first begin to practice fasting, it is very difficult to make it through the day. So strong is the habit of responding to the stimulus of hunger that it is practically impossible to overcome it. With practice, though, it gets much easier. Those of us who practice fasting regularly, especially longer fasts, become free from the dictates of hunger and can work all day without losing focus on our work by the distraction of hunger.

The primary purpose of fasting is to teach us about freedom. By fasting, we learn that it is possible to overcome the stimulus/response mechanism and begin to let our wisdom guide our actions. There are many other approaches that help us to learn about freedom, but the important point is to understand the stimulus/response mechanism. Then we will begin to experience freedom from things that we previously thought impossible to change our reactions to.

With guidance, true freedom is attainable; but, until you get there it is beyond your wildest dreams. Mahatma Ghandi said that you are truly free when your wisdom guides every reaction, including those reactions you thought were impossible. He proved his point by having an appendix operation with no anesthetic. During the operation he held a conversation as if the stimulus of pain was not even there.[1]

Many people confuse such stories with the idea that he just blocked out the pain. Although there is partial truth to the idea, history is full of people who say that they felt the pain just as much or more; but, their wisdom allowed them to control how they reacted to it. In Ghandi's case, he knew the pain was for his benefit and that the wise thing to do was to not pull away. He also had the wisdom to pull away when touching a hot stove.

If Ghandi was free to choose how to react to the stimulus of pain, why do we allow ourselves to be controlled by what other people say or the countless circumstances that influence our behavior? Once we start practicing freedom and gaining wisdom, we find the ability to control our reactions to every condition we experience in life. *Bipolar In Order* means to be free to react with wisdom to even the deepest depression or strongest stimulus of mania.

It may sound impossible to achieve the level of freedom that I am talking about, but that does not make it so. We have it within ourselves to gain freedom from simple things and, over time, expand that freedom to areas beyond our

---

1 Yogananda, Paramahansa, Autobiography of a Yogi, 1993, Self-Realization Fellowship, CA, p. 500

original limitations. Eventually, we could attain the level of control Ghandi and many others have shown us is possible. Even if we do not take it that far, we can enjoy a level of freedom that surpasses what we thought possible. Our wisdom guided actions will change how we relate to others and the world at large.

Those who have achieved true freedom have all said that it is within everyone's grasp. Who are we to believe--the naysayers who have not made the effort, or those of us who have direct experience of freedom and its effect on our lives? We may all be born with the right to be free, but in most circumstances that freedom is something that we must earn.

True freedom means to be able to choose the right way to respond to every stimulus, including depression, mania, hallucinatory, and delusional states. No longer controlled by our condition, our thoughts and actions are guided by our wisdom rather than being slaves to circumstance, habit, and low expectations.

The sections on *What Is In Our Way* and *How to Get There* will go into greater detail on how to achieve true freedom. For now, exposure to the idea is enough. You can begin by accepting that a greater freedom is possible even if you must put some limits on its full achievement.

Real Stability

"Stability is not immobility."
- *Klemens Von Metternich*[1]

The mainstream meaning of stability in depression, mania, hallucination, and delusion is to be in remission of symptoms for an extended period with the goal of being symptom free forever.[2] While I side with those who believe traditional tools including medicine and therapy are valid, I take issue with the goal itself. A stability that has us living a diminished life in fear of a relapse is only the beginning, not the end point, on the path from "disorder" to "in order." If stability is the goal, we need to redefine what it means and how we measure it.

When we look at the physical world, the dictionary defines stable as "not likely to give way or overturn; firmly fixed."[3] Stability means to be able to perform the intended action under duress. A race car with a low center of gravity is more stable while turning a corner than a minivan with a heavy load on the roof. While turning a corner, the driver of a minivan has to be careful so as not to flip the vehicle over. The race car driver needs to be careful too, but he has a vehi-

---

1 http://thinkexist.com/quotes/klemens_von_metternich/

2 Perlis, R.H.,Evidence-based strategies for achieving treatment goals in bipolar disorder: A review and synthesis of contemporary treatment guidelines., Journal of Current Psychosis and Theraputic Reports, V 1, N2 December, 2003, Massachusetts General Hospital, Boston.

3 New Oxford American Dictionary, 2nd Edition,

cle built for speed and agility, not for lumbering through a parking lot loaded down with camping gear on the roof.

In the mental world, the dictionary defines stable as "sane and sensible; not easily upset or disturbed."[1] Since the extremes of depression, mania, hallucination, and delusion typically accompany clear signs of being "upset or disturbed," it is understandable how freedom from symptoms became the standard definition of stability. Unfortunately, it forces us into a predicament--if our condition changes in the slightest bit, we become unstable because we cannot function under the duress. We live in fear that our condition might "turn the corner" and we will "flip out."

If you park the race car and the minivan in the garage they are both stable, but that is not the purpose of having a car. The same can be said of people. It might be necessary at first to achieve such a limited stability because anything else is too dangerous, but it can hardly be considered the end-point of treatment. I don't want to park my mind in the garage.

Having no highs or lows isn't stable, it is boredom! We need contrast in our lives. The problem is not highs and lows, it is our inability to have wisdom guided reactions to them. Stability needs to be seen as a range where our reactions are still within our control.

Real Stability means to maintain control in an ever wider range of experience. Over time we can gain stability in a range of highs and lows that would be considered "nor-

---

1 New Oxford American Dictionary, 2nd Edition,

mal" for people without our condition. With guidance, effort, and wisdom, we can even reach a level of stability beyond that of "normal" people. Some of us can even achieve stability across the entire range of the bipolar condition and live an extraordinary life.

Those who have carefully considered their experience with depression can validate the idea of stability. When we were first depressed it seemed unbearable. As we experience it more and more it gets easier to handle, at least at lower levels. As we experience deeper depressions, our ability to handle the lesser ones becomes stronger. Eventually we realize that the level that was first unbearable is now very easy to handle.

Eventually, we get to the point that our understanding is greater than most. When others experience situations that depress them, they turn to us because we are comfortable talking about it. Depression becomes our expertise. We can bring real stability to our own lives as well as help others to better understand their condition and become stable too.

Everyone gets depressed from time to time. It is very normal at lower levels and we understand that without the contrast of ups and downs life would be dull. Sooner or later we all have a situation that causes deep feelings of depression. The loss of a loved one or another great tragedy can put us in a state of true situational depression that lasts weeks or months, sometimes even years.

Those of us who have clinical depression go through a much deeper state. It is so much more intense on every level that it is impossible for those who have not had the experience to even comprehend how intense it is. Although most choose to avoid such states at all costs, those of us who choose to learn from the experience instead of just avoiding it gain insight that makes it easier for us.

The same trajectory of increased stability happens with hallucinations and delusions for those of us who choose to understand them. We find that they no longer control our reactions and we can remain stable in states that would completely disable others.

Mania is much more difficult for many to understand. As their experience has been horrible, they are in such fear of mania that they refuse to accept even the possibility of maintaining stability while manic. In my talks I can go into great detail about depression, but if I mention even the slightest mania some people get very upset. So terrible are their experiences and so horrifying the stories of manic people causing havoc that they consider it dangerous to even mention the possibility of getting it under control.

Nonetheless, many people have found themselves capable of maintaining stability in low levels of mania. They have developed the awareness and necessary support system to help them avoid the higher levels that they cannot control. Just as there are levels of freedom including those that most would consider impossible, it is within us to be able to get depression, mania, hallucination, and delusion under control in much greater levels than you can imagine.

Limiting our life to a very narrow range of emotions and experiences in fear that we may have a relapse is not stability at all. "Avoidance therapy" will never "cure" mania or depression, it will only force you into a diminished life with constant fear of relapse. Only by gaining insight, developing freedom from the dictates of our conditions, and finding real stability can we begin to live an advantaged life of *Self-Mastery* and *Equanimity*.

Self-Mastery

"I have come to measure spiritual advancement, not alone by the light that surrounds one when he meditates or by the visions he has of the saints, but by what he is able to endure in the hard cold light of day."
- Sister Gyanamata[1]

Self-mastery is *Clear Insight*, *True Freedom*, and *Real Stability* in action. You have attained self-mastery when every word and deed is based on doing the right thing instead of habits or emotion. Self-mastery is the overwhelming desire to act better today than yesterday.

Self-mastery requires introspection. I covered a basic technique for introspection in *The Bipolar Advantage* book.[2] The process is an easy way to become more aware of our thoughts and actions as well as the events that trigger them.

The steps to simple introspection include creating a list of questions to ask ourselves, nightly review of those questions, and use of the subconscious mind to monitor our thoughts and behaviors. We create five to seven questions each about our thoughts, actions, and spiritual life. Each question needs to have a "yes" or "no" answer so that it is a simple process during our nightly review. During the day, the subconscious mind monitors our every thought and action so that it can answer the questions at night. With regular practice, the thoughts and events that trigger our behaviors

---

1 God Alone, Selections from the letters of Sister Gyanamata, 1984, Self-Realization Fellowship, CA, p.181

2 Wootton, Tom, The Bipolar Advantage, 2005, Bipolar Advantage Publishers, CA p.68-81

become conscious and we find that we can choose the right response. Simple introspection is a powerful tool on the path to self-mastery.

While simple introspection can help us to better understand ourselves and our reactions to circumstances, real introspection is what it takes to achieve self-mastery. Self-mastery comes when we introspect continuously. No longer reliant on subconscious processes, we are consciously monitoring our thoughts and behaviors. We find that every action is preceded by a thought, even those we once believed to be automatic responses to stimuli. We decide to take the best response based on the insight gained in previous experiences. We may not always succeed, but with each attempt, our options become more clear and we develop the wisdom to make the right decision for the circumstance.

One of the early insights that comes from introspection is recognition of our tendency to excuse our behavior with justifications. Even when we know our actions to be wrong, we justify them by claiming that they were a reaction to what someone else did or some other outside influence. Self-mastery means there are no excuses for our behavior. We understand that no matter what the circumstance, we have the wisdom and willpower to do the right thing.

Occasionally I see a bumper sticker that says, "What would Jesus do?" I wonder if the sentiment is merely a platitude or an ideal the driver truly wants to live up to. Before every word or action, we need to ask ourselves if what we are thinking is in line with our own ideals. After every event, we need to analyze what we did and determine a better response for the next time we are confronted with a similar circumstance. When "What would I do" becomes the same as "What would Jesus do," we have fully attained self-mastery.

Many people try to justify their lack of willpower by saying that we are not Jesus and therefore cannot live up to his example. I have searched far and wide through the Bible and other religious texts and have not found anything to suggest such an attitude. In fact, scripture speaks of following his example. We have to take responsibility for our failings, but should never lower the bar for what is possible or stop trying to improve.

In the depths of his deepest struggle, Jesus rose above the darkness and the pain. He put his own suffering aside and forgave the very ones who were putting him to death. "Father, forgive them for they know not what they do."[1] His action is our example of what Jesus would do and exactly how he addressed an outside trigger. We most certainly will not attain that level of self-mastery easily or quickly, but it is an attainable goal and we should strive for nothing less.

Long before Jesus was born, Patanjali wrote the *Yoga Sutras*,[2] otherwise known as the "noble eightfold path." These eight steps outline the highest or "royal" path to enlightenment with references to the *Mahabarata*[3] and the *Bha-*

---

1 Luke 23:34

2 Swami Vivekananda, The Yoga-Sutras of Patanjali: The Essential Yoga Texts for Spiritual Enlightenment, Translation, 2007 Watkins, London

3 Smith, J.D., The Mahabharata, 2009, Abridged ed., Penguin Classics, NY

vagad Gita,[1] which recount events dating as early as 5,000 years ago. The foundation of the "royal" path is self-mastery.

The eight steps on the path include Yama (things you should do), Niyama (things you shouldn't do), Asana (discipline of the body), Pranayama (life force control), Pratyhara (withdrawal of all senses), Dharana (concentration), Dhyana (meditation), and Samadhi (oneness, enlightenment, ecstasy, equanimity). Without the foundation of self-mastery, it is not possible to reach the ultimate goal. Many people think that they can just skip over self-mastery (yama/niyama, the Ten Commandments) and meditate their way to enlightenment, but thousands of years of experience says otherwise.

Self-mastery is as much a path as a destination. We must constantly work on personal growth and judge our progress not in comparison to others, but to our own past. If we are going to become masters of our own lives, we need to set clear and measurable goals as outlined in the *How To Get There* section and constantly assess whether we are justifying our current thoughts and actions.

Justification takes many forms: excusing our behavior because someone else acts badly, blaming our actions on circumstances, and, worst of all, for those with mental conditions, claiming that our condition has ultimate power over our actions. Do we really think our condition is somehow harder to overcome than the problems and difficulties the saints from all religions faced? Is our pain somehow worse than so many others throughout history that overcame their hardships? While we have exceptional challenges, the an-

---

1 Yogananda,Paramahansa, The Bhavagad Gita, translation, 2003 Self-Realization Fellowship, CA

swer is no. Our challenges do not prevent us from achieving self-mastery. From my perspective, we succeed in part *because* of our condition.

Self-mastery is available to everyone who makes the effort. In the final analysis, how we act is the only valid criteria for anyone who claims that his/her condition is under control. Too many people are claiming that they don't need help when their behavior says otherwise. Far worse, too many are saying that you should follow their advice when their own results betray the effectiveness of their claims. If you cannot point out clear and measurable improvements over the last year and clear goals as outlined in the *How To Get There* section, you are not on the path to self-mastery.

The world seems designed to help us on the path to self-mastery. As soon as we think we have something mastered, we are confronted with an opportunity to prove it. We all have someone in our lives whose behavior really bothers us. He or she may be a work colleague, a classmate, a friend, or a family member. That person may no longer be a part of your life, but you will continue to be challenged by individuals with the same mannerisms until you have learned how to handle that behavior in others. Even after you do figure it out, people with those same behaviors will keep showing up just to make sure you haven't slipped. It is a law of the universe.

A great way to make sure you still have it under control is the Grocery Store Test™.[1] When you pick a line at the grocery store because you think it is going to be the fastest

---

1 The Grocery Store Test always gets a laugh at my talks, probably because we have all failed the test repeatedly and know it.

one, it turns into the slowest. Your mind starts thinking, "I wish that lady would quit fumbling in her purse and just pay the bill" or "If the clerk would shut up and scan faster I could get out of here." Those kind of thoughts lead to behaviors that are often far less than self-mastery if we don't learn to recognize them and change. When we can remain calm and help everyone else in line to calm down too, we have exhibited self-mastery and made a positive change in the world.

Equanimity

"Be steadfast in yoga, devotee. Perform your duty without attachment, remaining equal to success or failure. Such equanimity of mind is called Yoga."
- Bhagavad-Gita[1]

The end point of stability is a state called "equanimity." Equanimity means even-minded under all conditions. When in equanimity, our wisdom guides all of our actions and we stop seeing one state as more valuable than any other. Disease and health, pain and pleasure, loss and gain,[2] or any of the dualities of the world cease to exist and we feel blissful in all circumstances.

Equanimity is often misunderstood to mean the same as the old definition of stability. Many people talk about achieving a state where there is only calmness, no ups or downs. They interpret it to mean being in a tranquil place that allows people to relax, to escape from the stresses and strains of everyday life and to "recharge their batteries." Although it is helpful to occasionally remove ourselves from the conditions that create stress for us as it helps us to achieve some peace, equanimity is the ability to remain peaceful while the world is crashing around us.

Equanimity goes by many names: ecstasy, bliss, samadhi, nirvana, self-realization, enlightenment, and many

1 Yogananda,Paramahansa, The Bhavagad Gita, translation, 2003 Self-Realization Fellowship, CA, 2:48

2 Yogananda, Paramahansa, The Autobiography of a Yogi, 1987, Self-Realization Fellowship, CA, p. 409

more. The state of equanimity is revered by all religions as the ultimate state of being. Often thought reserved for only the saints to experience, the saints themselves say that it is within every one of us to experience it.

Many of the greatest people in history have achieved equanimity through the same states that we are told to avoid. Many even credit deep depression as one of the clearest paths to get there. In *The Depression Advantage*[1] I detailed how Saint Francis, Saint Teresa of Avila, Saint John of the Cross, Saint Anthony of the Desert, and Milerepa all found equanimity through depression. Equanimity for them was the result of facing their condition and learning from it instead of avoiding it. Saint John of the Cross even wrote a book called *The Dark Night of the Soul*[2] that details the ways that depression is a divine path.

Equanimity as applied to depression does not mean we are never depressed. It means that although we are having symptoms that indicate depression, we are unaffected by them. Equanimity means *True Freedom, Real Stability*, and wisdom guided responses to all conditions.

Depression has four main components, physical, mental, emotional, and spiritual. Not all states are the same, but if we pay enough attention we can see that all four components are involved to some degree. There are three main levels of depression: normal ups and downs, situational depression, and clinical depression. It is commonly believed that as we progress from normal levels to deep

---

1 Wootton, Tom, The Depression Advantage, 2007 Bipolar Advantage Publishers, CA

2 Peers, E. Allison, The Dark Night of the Soul, translation, 1990 Random House, N.Y.

clinical depression the risk of suicide increases, but that is a very simplistic view.

Some people commit suicide at levels of depression that are not that deep. Others go into very deep depressions without ever even thinking about it. Some attempt suicide at one level of depression and then go to much deeper levels and don't even consider it. There is no magical point that causes suicide attempts. It is different for every individual.

My own experience with depression illustrates this principle. As I got older my depressions got much deeper and more frequent. My understanding increased, yet I was still debilitated by them and was even in great danger of suicide.

Several years ago I was in a very deep depression during a vacation in Cancun with my family. Although the physical pain was not so great, the mental component got the best of me. My mind was stuck in a loop that was a combination of obsessive thoughts and visions of my own death. The spiritual crisis was that life had no meaning and was not worth living. My symptoms were much more complex, of course, but the thoughts about killing myself were what did me in.

It is not necessary to go into more detail to make the point, but suffice it to say I remember it like it happened this morning. One thing about intense experiences of any kind: they become deeply embedded in our memory.

One positive outcome of my suicide attempt is that I began to pay very close attention to my depressions and began to understand them very deeply. I chose to analyze the symptoms and try to become expert in both the experience and the choices of how to react to them. As I learned more about myself and my condition, I slowly gained power over depression. I found that I could handle the lesser states easily and could even function acceptably in states that could clearly be compared to situational depression for "normal" people.

My understanding helped me to write *The Depression Advantage*[1] and give great detail of the various levels of depression. Yet, I was still a long way from being able to see it in the light that the saints mentioned. During that time I was also functioning better and better, although my state was a fairly deep depression. I was thinking that I was "rising above" the pain and wrote about how the saints had done the same thing.

Life is not as simple as having a "breakthrough" that changes everything, but there are highlights that stick out and can seem like "breakthrough moments." Mine came during a keynote talk that I was giving for San Bernardino County Mental Health Department's annual dinner. As I was waiting for the event to start and setting up the recording equipment, I realized that I was in a state almost exactly the same as the one that nearly took my life in Cancun.

I am one of the rare people who have no fear of public speaking and usually don't even give it a thought. This time I was extremely nervous about my ability to give the talk

---

1 Wootton, Tom, The Depression Advantage, 2007 Bipolar Advantage Publishers, CA

and so was my wife Ellen. Right up to the very second that I was called, I had serious doubts that I could even stand up.

As I stood up to face the crowd, I started off telling them that I was having the deepest depression of my life and was not sure how it would go, but was going to give it a try. I related my story about Cancun and proceeded to go to my usual speaking points.

As I got into a groove, my fear went away while the symptoms of depression actually increased. My paranoia told me I was doing a horrible job, yet the video and reaction of the crowd said it went pretty well. It may not have been my best talk ever, but it was good enough for some of it to have made it to our YouTube Channel![1]

My experiences previous to my "breakthrough talk" was the basis for my thoughts about insight, freedom, and stability because I was directly experiencing the benefits of the wisdom that I was gaining. I was also talking about the possibility of equanimity even though my own experiences of it was fleeting at best. My breakthrough was that I could maintain some semblance of equanimity in extreme states and still perform my responsibilities.

My ability to experience the most intense depressions and choose how to react to it rapidly increased after my breakthrough. I would wake up in the morning in such extreme states that I could see how depression could so easily kill someone, yet was finding it oddly interesting. I was so excited about the experience that my behavior was confus-

---

1 http://www.youtube.com/BipolarAdvantage

ing those around me. In a manner that would suggest I won the lottery, I told my friend Peter Russell that I was in the deepest depression of my life.

Peter was so confused by my behavior that he asked me if there was such a thing as a "mixed state" where we are part depressed and part manic. When I said that it is a common occurrence he was visibly relieved. The next day he confirmed the existence of "mixed states" with Ellen. When Ellen shared the conversation with me, I realized that I was in uncharted territory.

It took several weeks to finally figure it out. It came to me as I was watching my cat jump up to a counter. Anyone with a cat knows that they jump exactly the right amount every time. I realized that I needed to adjust my reactions to both mania and depression much the same way a cat jumps from one place to another. My first cat-like move was when I was deeply depressed. I set out to jump from waking up in a depression that previously had me bedridden, or worse, to behavior so normal no one would know unless I told them.

When my next manic episode came, I found that I could make the same adjustments that I apply to depressive episodes. I found that I was truly experiencing equanimity in all states and not valuing one over the other. I was also functioning the same no matter what state I was in.

I began to realize that the saints didn't "rise above the pain" or make it go away. They got to a point that they were experiencing it fully, but the pain was no longer controlling their reactions.

The death of my dog was the final piece of the puzzle for me. We had Kriya for 14 years and were both very close to her. She had struggled with cancer for the last couple years of her life, and finally one day could not handle it any longer. The doctor examined her and said, "Have you thought about end of life for her?" I looked over at Ellen, then back to the doctor, and said, "Is there anything you can do to remove Kriya's pain for a while so that we can prepare for it?" I knew that we needed to be there for it and that it was going to take some preparation to be able to face it.

Holding Kriya during the procedure was exquisitely painful, but was also very beautiful for me. I was so moved by the experience that I found profound meaning in having been through it.

The Depression Advantage should not be misunderstood as the ability to "rise above" the pain. The advantage is that we have the ability to experience it more deeply, while having the wisdom to choose how to react.

It is impossible to have a life worth living that completely eliminates depression. The "cure" for depression is not the removal of all symptoms. The "cure" is to get to the point that the symptoms lose their power over us. We cannot get to that point by avoiding it. Equanimity means that even though the symptoms are still there, we no longer see them as negative.

I have been repeating a quote by Saint Teresa of Avila[1] almost constantly for 8 months now; "The pain is still there.

---

1 Teresa of Avila: Mystical Writings, ed. Tessa Bielecki, 1999, Crossword Publishing Company, NY. p. 119

It bothers me so little now that I feel my soul is served by it."
I recently realized that she didn't actually say that. She said,
"The pain is still there. It bothers me so little now that I feel
the Lord is served by it." In subconsciously translating it to
fit my beliefs, I missed that the reference to "me" meant
"soul," not the reference to God, as in "the Lord is served by
it." I believe that the soul is God within, so in trying to inter-
nalize the quote, I did it in a way that missed the deeper
truth.

One of the things I have been sorting through is that
Saint Teresa was clearly affected by her condition. There
were long periods where she was bedridden and in extreme
pain. What I have learned from Saint Teresa is that my body,
mind, and emotions may be very bothered, but when I focus
on my soul I am in bliss. From equanimity (bliss) I can see
that pain is part of bliss just as much as pleasure, happiness,
and all other conditions.

Central to my beliefs is that every moment of our
lives is an opportunity to be in bliss, but we avoid those with
the most potential because we think that the difficult experiences need to be removed first. We are closer to experiencing
bliss during the difficult times, not further from it. For most
of us, we mistakenly think bliss means happiness. We cannot
truly know bliss until we see it in our pain. Once we find
bliss in pain, we find it everywhere. I now interpret Teresa's
quote as: "The pain is still there. It doesn't bother my soul at
all and helps me to be in bliss."

It takes equanimity to fully understand how bipolar
or depression can be seen as an advantage. Once we begin to
look at depression and mania from the perspective of equa-

nimity, we see how such richness of experience brings insight and understanding that is beyond the capacity for those without such a perspective to even imagine.

Perspective

Life becomes clearer when seen from a higher perspective.

When I was vice president of U-Haul of Northern California, we occasionally heard that we should include Alaska in our network. When asked why, agents would say, "We get calls for trucks to Alaska all the time." Research revealed we didn't get that many calls and certainly not enough to justify the cost. Since Alaska was exotic and outside of the norm, our reservation agents placed more significance on the request and perceived it as happening more frequently than it really was. The actual numbers gave us a proper perspective and helped us make clear decisions.

My U-Haul experience taught me a lot about perspective that I find useful when thinking about mental health. For example, those who have one or a few hallucinations during their life place tremendous significance on them. The hallucinations are often seen as visits from God or seminal events in their lives. Those who hallucinate all the time and have not developed insight, believe it when they are told to keep the hallucinations from occurring. Those who have understanding, see them for what they really are--simply one aspect of experience that is neither more nor less significant

---

1 http://www.quotegarden.com/perspective.html

than any other. With the proper perspective of understanding, we can choose to react to all experiences based on the wisdom gained from greater insight.

The current paradigm is that we are incapable of understanding our condition and should avoid it at all costs. The belief is if we get too close to the edge we will surely fall off, just as so many others have. What we fail to see is that we sent people out with no training, guidance, or understanding. Of course they got lost. Just as in Columbus' day, sailors went out without knowledge and understanding and they got lost. The lost sailors inadvertently proved the erroneous assumption that the world was flat, just as those with mental conditions in "disorder" prove the danger of getting outside of a very narrow range.

The majority of people want to have a deeper experience of life. If given the choice between a limited life or one that is rich and varied, almost everyone will pick the rich and varied option. Of course, some will pick the limited life, but mostly due to fear. If given a life where your thoughts are slowed down, your senses are diminished, and your reactions to the world are minimized, you will quickly understand why the majority of people that are overmedicated do not stick with the prescription. We want more life, not less.

The advantage Columbus had is that he saw the world from the other side and knew that it was not as everyone feared. My advantage is that I have seen the inner world from the other side and have a unique perspective to share.

The Current Perspective

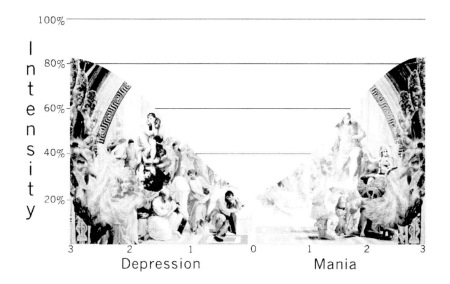

If we were to graph our moods based on how intense they are it would look something like the above. As we move further towards the extremes of depression or mania, our level of perceived intensity increases. Of course, it is much more complex than a simple graph, but the point is that there are different levels of intensity that can be tied to our experiences.

I wrote at length about the ranges in *The Depression Advantage*,[1] so I won't go into detail here. Suffice it to say that as the level of intensity increases, the odds increase of attempted suicide and other negative consequences, at least in untrained people.

---

1 Wootton, Tom, The Depression Advantage, 2007 Bipolar Advantage Publishers, CA, p.51-66

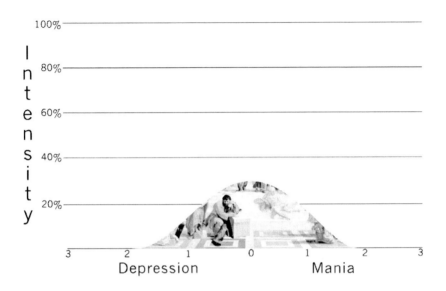

The common belief is that as we become more depressed, manic, hallucinatory, or delusional, the intensity becomes too much for us to handle. The need for narrowing our range is precipitated by behaviors that range from inappropriate to life threatening. Some bipolar people in crisis need to be kept in the zero range because they can't even handle normal intensity without losing control.

The recovery goals of the current paradigm of treating mental illness, including use of current medications, is to lower the intensity of all symptoms.[1] Therapy teaches us to recognize and avoid triggers. Avoidance of difficult situations keeps our experiences in a very narrow range, but the goal of even "avoidance-based" therapy should be to help people to live within the range of "normal" people.

---

1 Perlis, R.H.,Evidence-based strategies for achieving treatment goals in bipolar disorder: A review and synthesis of contemporary treatment guidelines., Journal of Current Psychosis and Theraputic Reports, V1N 2 December, 2003, Massachusetts General Hospital, Boston.

As you will read in the section on *How To Get There*, the first step of treatment is to narrow the range of moods and other symptoms until we are stable. My perspective is that the narrow range is a necessary starting point, but not the end of the path. Once we are trained and capable of handling the narrow range, we can begin to expand that range and experience life more fully. Eventually we can expand the range in ways that were previously considered impossible.

The Monastic Perspective

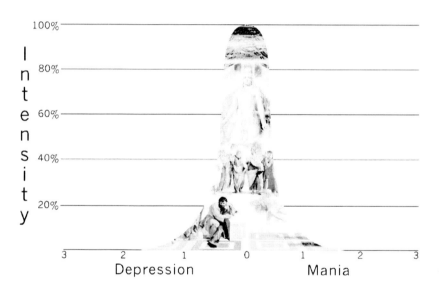

A perspective that I came to understand from my years in a monastery is one that influences me to this day. Secluding ourselves from the hustle and bustle of everyday life, we spent many hours practicing disciplines that helped focus the mind so that we could live more in the moment.

The combination of a peaceful environment and the fellowship of like-minded souls helped us develop the willpower to overcome all obstacles in our path. The monastic belief is that all distractions must be minimized in order to have a more intense spiritual experience.

While I was in the monastery, I minimized my range of experience so that I could develop a deeper spiritual life. This practice is commonly used in all major religions and is the reason they have monastic traditions. They find it easier to keep focused on the goal that they value more than anything else. This belief is the reason for abstinence in the priesthood of the Catholic Church, for example.

The value of limiting the range of experience cannot be understated. It has proven to be an effective path for both spiritual adherents and in the treatment of mental disorders. There is a tremendous track record of success with limiting experience in order to achieve a stability that allows us to survive.

But minimizing distractions is just as limiting as the proven track record which kept the sailors in Columbus' day from venturing beyond a narrow range from shore. Both are fear based beliefs that confine us to a world much smaller than what is available to us. They are based on experiments that only strive to prove the predetermined objective.

One outcome of my spiritual practice was the belief that avoidance of things that triggered thoughts and emotions outside of a narrow range was the necessary path to my goals. It took the perspective of bipolar to understand that I was imposing a serious limitation on my ability to have a truly full life.

The New Perspective

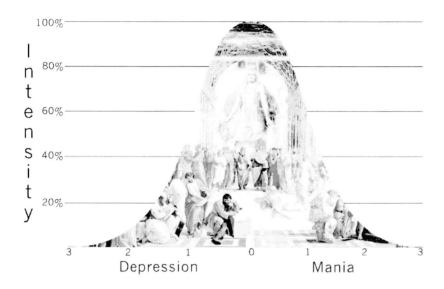

The above graph illustrates the beginning of a path to a more advantaged life. By expanding the range while keeping the intensity, it can be argued that we gain more of our goal; having rich experiences and more of them.

In this case, we have expanded our range of experiences to mirror those that "normal" people have, while still maintaining stability. Combined with the monastic practice of focus (an important mind skill), we will eventually get to a state where we are experiencing the range of a "normal" person , but with much higher intensity.

By applying the concept of equanimity to this extended range, we can experience the entire range as equally valuable and let our wisdom guide our response to the various stimuli that previously broke our stability.

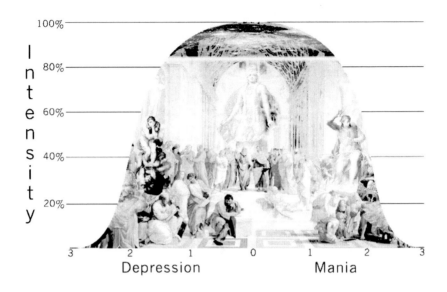

The next level of expanded range includes the experiences at the outside edge where "normal" people lose stability. At first, we may not be able to experience it fully or keep our reactions completely guided by our wisdom, but we are growing to a range of experience unheard of by most. As we gain understanding and skills, we find that we can comfortably live in this expanded range while acting well within the boundaries of acceptable behavior. Eventually we can get to full intensity of experience while maintaining self-mastery and equanimity.

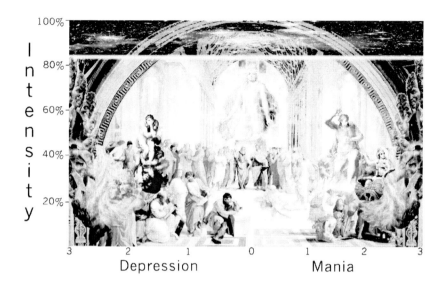

We get our first glimpse of "the other side" when we begin to understand the furthest reaches of experience. This is the part that generates tremendous fear in those who cling to the old beliefs. So many people have fallen off the edge that we believe it to be a law of the universe. Just like in Columbus' day, people today are convinced that the world is as we believe it to be.

As we develop understanding, discipline, mind skills, and wisdom, we begin to be able to function even in extreme states of depression, mania, hallucination, and delusion. Our range of experience at this point is beyond the ability to comprehend by all but a few people who have been there.

Once we find that we can function in these extreme ranges of experience, we begin to develop a completely new perspective.

We fully realize the Bipolar Advantage when we reach equanimity across the entire range of experience. Once there, it becomes as obvious as the new world was to Columbus; we see the ignorance in the old paradigm.

If the goal in life is to live it more fully, which has the advantage?

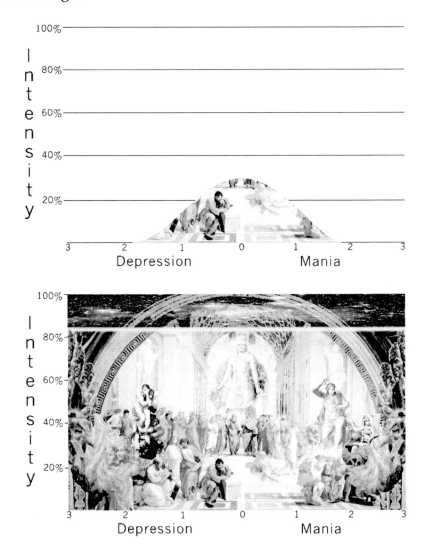

Once our lives are "in order," we have a whole new perspective. Like the story of Christopher Columbus, until we see the other side, we have a hard time believing that the world is not as others tell us. I fully understand why people view depression, mania, hallucination, and delusion as just "illnesses" or "disorders." They have not yet seen the other side or believe it to be possible. Without the perspective of experience, they cannot understand why I see it differently.

This perspective shines a much clearer light on the idea that mental states can be an advantage. Once our lives are "in order," depression, mania, hallucination, delusion, and the many mixed states in between can be tremendous advantages in our lives. The experiences become something that would be sorely missed if we had to go without them. Once "in order," it is clearly an advantage to have our condition.

When we see the whole picture, we understand how the parts fit together into a beautiful work of art.

Image collage from Renaissance paintings by Raphael and Michelangelo, Bhagavad Gita illustrations, and Hubble Telescope image by E. N. for BPA. Color web images at: www.bipolarinorder.com

What Is In The Way

When Columbus set sail in search of the new world, he had already done the hardest part. He had overcome his own fears and challenged the dominant beliefs of his time. He had persuaded many other people to take a huge risk at a time when everyone thought his goals were crazy. He created a plan, found support, built a team, and set sail into uncharted waters.

One might credibly argue that Columbus and his team faced tremendous hardships during the voyage that made it the hardest part of the whole affair. Yet he wouldn't have even faced them without first challenging the beliefs that were in the way.

In a similar way, there are several beliefs that are in the way of achieving *Results Worth Striving For*. Some of these beliefs are embedded in the model of mental illness and must be challenged.

"In the way" beliefs include the very definitions of depression, mania, hallucination, and delusion themselves. Also on the list are the belief that mental conditions are a disability or an illness, that it is a mood disorder instead of a behavior disorder, and that our situation is somehow special.

It is easy to dismiss the ideas in this section as delusional without considering the possibility that there may be some truth in them. Just as everyone thought that Columbus was "crazy," far too many will choose to label me as "crazy" so they do not have to face their own fears or wrestle with their own misconceptions.

The definition of insanity is often joked about as "doing the same thing over and over expecting different results." Clinging to the old beliefs is clearly not working. Refusing to consider that our beliefs may be part of the problem is certainly insane. Perhaps it takes a "crazy" person to help redefine what it means to live with a mental condition.

The Definitions Are Not Definitive

Words, and the meaning we place on them, have tremendous influence over how we experience the things that they define. In Sanskrit, the oldest language in the world, the sound of the word itself influences how we perceive the object or idea that it defines.[1] The Eskimos have eight different words for snow.[2] Is it safe to assume that snow for the Eskimos is at least eight times more complex than for most of us?

Some have gone so far as to say that without a word for something we cannot experience it. The book *No Word for Time: The Way of the Algonquin People* explores how without a reference in vocabulary, the people don't even notice the passage of time.[3]

Mystics describe the states that they attain as ineffable, meaning too great or extreme to be expressed or described in words. In *Deautomatization and the Mystic Experience*, Arthur J. Deikman wrote about how our perceptions change when we stop automatically putting words to them. He described the experience as being richer and more mean-

---

1 Russell, Peter and Shearer, A., The Upanishads, translation, 1989, Unwin Hyman Ltd., London, p. 8

2 http://users.utu.fi/freder/Pullum-Eskimo-VocabHoax.pdf - this myth has been disproved, yet as most still believe it, I use it here as a metaphor.

3 Pritchard, Evan, No Word for Time: The Way of the Algonquin People, 2nd edition, 2001, Council Oaks Books, San Francisco

ingful to those who have deautomatization episodes, no matter what caused them.[1]

The words "depression," "mania," "hallucination," "delusion," and "schizoaffective" are loaded with meanings that flavor our experience. The very definitions of the terms color our perceptions of these conditions in profound ways. By defining what it means to have a particular condition, we are limited in our ability to understand what is really happening. Freeing ourselves from the influence of the words can help us to have a richer and more meaningful experience.

Depression

The following are descriptions typically associated with depression.[2] Not everyone who is depressed experiences every symptom. Some people express a few symptoms, while others have many. Severity of symptoms varies with individuals and also varies over time.

- Persistent sad, anxious, or "empty" mood
- Feelings of hopelessness, pessimism
- Feelings of guilt, worthlessness, helplessness
- Loss of interest or pleasure in hobbies and activities that were once enjoyed, including sex
- Decreased energy, fatigue, being "slowed down"
- Difficulty concentrating, remembering, or making decisions

---

1 Deikman, A. "Deautomatization and the Mystic Experience." Understanding Mysticism. Image Books: Garden City, 1980

2 http://psychcentral.com/lib/2006/types-and-symptoms-of-depression/ - While many websites have similar descriptions, Psych Central is a favorite site and well worth visiting.

◯ Insomnia, early-morning awakening, or oversleeping
◯ Appetite and/or weight loss or overeating and weight gain
◯ Thoughts of death or suicide; suicide attempts
◯ Restlessness, irritability
◯ Persistent physical symptoms that do not respond to treatment, such as headaches, digestive disorders, and chronic pain

When I was first diagnosed, I was influenced by this list of traits that "define" depression. Like most people, I was afraid of depression and wanted nothing more than to make it go away. I didn't recognize the power the definition had over me until years later when my perspective had changed.

Upon achieving some equanimity and the perspective of depression "in order," I began to look much deeper at how the definition was influencing my perceptions. I am starting to separate my experience of depression from my reactions to it. I am beginning to realize that I have a choice in how to react to depressive states.

There appears to be a false linkage between depressions and reactions in the descriptions, as well as value judgements that make us see our experiences only negatively. Many of the descriptions that make up this definition may not be actual symptoms, but instead are common reactions to them. There is a big difference--while symptoms may be unavoidable, we can choose to react in positive ways instead of the ones listed.

Look through the list again and try to see what I mean. The most obvious ones:

○ "Thoughts of death or suicide; suicide attempts" - thoughts of suicide and death are common, who says it has to lead to suicide attempts?

○ "Restlessness, irritability" - even when feeling restless, can't the choice be made to not be so irritable?

○ "Appetite and/or weight loss or overeating and weight gain" - if insight says that while depressed weight gain is probable, can't wisdom be used to choose a healthier diet?

The hard ones:

○ "Difficulty concentrating, remembering, or making decisions" - depends on what I am concentrating on or trying to remember; I remember my deepest depressions more than any other experiences in life. Memory is associated with intensity. Tying something to remember to the intense state of depression embeds it so that it will not be easily forgotten.

○ "Feelings of hopelessness, pessimism" and "Feelings of guilt, worthlessness, helplessness" - are these reactions to depression colored by negative valuation of the experience?

Depression for me is really the experience of pain: physical, mental, emotional, and spiritual. What meaning I derive from it, values I place on it, and how I choose to act are my reactions to it.

I know that this is a very difficult concept to accept. It challenges everything we have been told. An illustration may help to make sense of it:

I am currently experiencing a very deep depression that has persisted for several months. The physical symptoms are extreme. My bones ache, I have severe and sharp muscle pain, my head is pounding, my eyes burn, my stomach feels nauseous, and despite the fatigue I am unable to sleep. The mental symptoms are equal if not stronger. I keep hallucinating myself committing suicide in infinite ways, voices keep telling me, "Kill yourself, nobody likes you, you are not worth living," and I am constantly with the thought that this will never go away. Emotionally, I am sad beyond words. I deeply remember the feelings of loss when my dog died and the grieving I was experiencing while recently visiting my mother in the hospital. I am in a state of spiritual despair. Life has no meaning, God does not exist, and I feel no connection whatsoever with the world. This depression feels every bit as deep as the time I tried to kill myself, if not more so.

My internal reaction to this depression is that I see this as the perfect time to write this part of the book. It is so exquisitely rich and detailed of an experience that the only word that fully describes it is beautiful. As I contemplate the beauty, I feel that I more deeply understand what Saint Francis meant when he renounced the Franciscan Order. He told his disciples that they missed the whole point when they expressed the desire to remove the pain he was experiencing at the end of his life.[1] Seeing the beauty is why Saint Teresa of Avila said, "The pain bothers me so little now that I feel my soul is served by it."[2]

---

1 Fulop-Miller, Rene, The Saints that Moved the World, Reprint ed. 1991, Ayer Co.Pub., N.H., p.263

2 Teresa of Avila: Mystical Writings, ed. Tessa Bielecki, 1999, Crossword Publishing Company, NY. p. 119

Along with the internal reaction, I have a choice of how to react externally. If the physical pain is not so over-whelming as to keep me bedridden, I can move about while recognizing my limitations. I would be foolish to compete in an athletic event and think I could perform at my best. My mental and emotional state demands that I am extra vigilant in monitoring myself to ensure that my responses to ordinary stressors are not being unduly influenced by my state of mind. My past experience tells me that contemplating the significance of the state is a fruitful time spiritually and could lead to valuable insights. I am also well aware that some of the insights may prove delusional when discussed with others.

I can make choices on how to act by considering all of the factors in discussions with members of my team. My actions may not be perfect, but with each new experience there is more information to use the next time I am faced with similar circumstances. By this process, I have experiential proof that depression and the reaction to it are not linked as the definition implies.

I have to be careful that I don't appear to value this experience more than the others in my life. I do not want people to mistake this as simply masochism or a perverse view of pain. It is important to point out that from the perspective of equanimity, all experiences are equally beautiful and valuable, even if completely different in their manifestations.

Mania

The following are descriptions typically associated with mania.[1] Not everyone who is manic experiences every symptom. Some people express a few symptoms, while others have many. Severity of symptoms varies with individuals and also varies over time.

- Abnormal or excessive elation
- Unusual irritability
- Decreased need for sleep
- Grandiose notions
- Increased talking
- Racing thoughts
- Increased sexual desire
- Markedly increased energy
- Poor judgment
- Inappropriate social behavior

Again, these definitions can be interpreted in different ways. Some of these could be seen as reactions instead of actual symptoms. Let's take a look at this list:

- "Abnormal or excessive elation" - what's wrong with that?
- "Unusual irritability" - just like in depression, we can choose not to be irritable. We have a choice in how to act.
- "Decreased need for sleep" - while this can be a great asset for productivity, it takes wisdom to make sure we are not burning our bodies out, and self-mastery

---

1 http://psychcentral.com/lib/2006/types-and-symptoms-of-depression/ - While many websites have similar descriptions, Psych Central is a favorite site and well worth visiting.

to ensure our decreased need for sleep doesn't cause a detriment to those around us.

○ "Grandiose notions" - some of the best ideas in the world came from grandiose thinking. It takes wisdom and shared insight with team members to recognize the ideas that have the best chance for success.

○ "Increased talking" - while increased talking in a shy person could be a good thing, self-mastery is the ability to recognize the appropriateness of all behaviors.

○ "Racing thoughts" - this can be an incredible asset, it's the reaction to our racing thoughts that can cause problems.

○ "Increased sexual desire" - while some cultures have a total aversion to anything sexual, there is nothing inherently wrong with having an increased sexual desire. It is inappropriate expressions of the desire that are the problem.

○ "Markedly increased energy" - just like decreased need for sleep, this can be a great thing. We need to monitor our health carefully and don't burn ourselves out.

○ "Poor judgment" and "inappropriate social behavior"- aren't these just a sign of lack of self-mastery, exacerbated by grandiose notions, racing thoughts, and increased sexual desire?

Based on wisdom, we are free to choose how to address many of the reactions related to mania. Once I developed enough self-mastery to choose how to react, I was able to begin to explore the positive aspects of mania without exhibiting the negative behaviors that can ruin so many lives. I began to recognize the false linkage that says mania automatically includes the negative reactions to it.

Since most people experience mania as out of control, it is easy to understand why it engenders such fear. It is much easier for people to accept depression "in order" than to even contemplate the possibility of mania being "in order." Nonetheless, if we are going to change the paradigm, it is necessary to present the case even if it will be argued against as forcefully as what Columbus had to endure. The only way to break through the fear is to tell people what it looks like from the other side, and persuade enough people to responsibly make the journey, until the evidence becomes overwhelming and the paradigm changes.

The common belief is that as we progress from normal highs and lows to hypomania, we get out of control and end up in full blown mania where it is impossible to function and are a great danger to ourselves and everyone around us. While this is clearly true for those who have never developed insight, freedom, stability, or self-mastery, it is not so for those of us who have the skills and awareness to be able to take advantage of the condition.

Many people may take this argument as an excuse to act irresponsibly and misperceive it as a license to let their mania go without taking responsibility for their actions. Like the deeper states of depression, this is not something to be explored without experienced guidance and close supervision as outlined in the *How To Get There* section.

Several months ago, I was in full blown mania for thirty days. This included physical, auditory, and visual hallucinations along with delusional thinking. With my wife, many clients and friends, along with several professionals as witnesses, I acted well within the bounds of acceptable behavior while accomplishing an inordinate amount of work. My behaviors were such that some thought I was just a little hypomanic, while most didn't even notice.

During that time, I conceived and created a new piece of software, started writing this book, rewrote our website, added several videos to our YouTube channel,[1] and accomplished many "things." From the American perspective that places great value on accomplishing "things," it was an incredibly productive time. From my perspective it was equally valuable as the aforementioned depression that produced tremendous insight.

After thirty days of mania I was starting to feel like it was taking too much of a toll on my body. Maintaining stability became increasingly difficult with each passing day. While my current depression has been going on for several months, I find that the length of time that I can experience mania is much more limited than that of depression. I find stability much more difficult to maintain during mania than even the deepest depression. For me, mania presents a greater danger. While it can be advantageous to have manic bursts where wonderfully creative ideas manifest, the manic state needs to be very tightly controlled. With that insight, I used Ativan®[2] along with lifestyle changes to come down after thirty days to a calmer state.

―――――――――――――――

1 http://www.youtube.com/BipolarAdvantage

2 Wyeth - http://www.wyeth.com/

Some will say that they prefer mania to depression. It is important to point out again that from the perspective of equanimity, all experiences are equally beautiful and valuable, even if completely different in their manifestations. It is not the situations that make us who we are; it is how we choose to react to those situations.

Hallucinations And Delusions

In speaking with several authorities, there is great confusion as to what role hallucinations and delusions play in bipolar, depression, and even schizophrenia. The definitions of schizoaffective, psychosis, and schizophrenia are very confusing and incredibly similar. Because of my diagnosis of bipolar and the fact that I have hallucinations and delusions, I have been diagnosed as "bipolar I schizoaffective." Adding to the confusion, there are other people with minor states of hypomania that are also considered "bipolar I schizoaffective." Even though we don't necessarily share the same intensity of our manic experiences, we are diagnosed the same simply because we share hallucinations. While I don't have a definitive answer for the confusion, it is important to look at how we think about these issues.

Schizoaffective Disorder

Schizoaffective Disorder is characterized by the presence of **one of the following**:[1]

◇ Major Depressive Episode (must include depressed mood)

---

1 http://psychcentral.com/disorders/sx4.htm - While many websites have similar descriptions, Psych Central is a favorite site and well worth visiting.

◇ Manic Episode
◇ Mixed Episode

As well as the presence of **at least two** of the following symptoms, for at least one month:

◇ Delusions
◇ Hallucinations
◇ Disorganized speech (e.g., frequent derailment or incoherence)
◇ Grossly **disorganized** or catatonic **behavior**
◇ **Negative symptoms** (e.g., affective flattening, alogia, avolition)

This definition is certainly one of the most confusing. If I have hallucinations that last only 29 days, am I not schizoaffective? What am I then?

While I recognize delusions and hallucinations as symptoms of my condition, is disorganized speech just a reaction to them? Sometimes when I hallucinate, I find it very difficult to remain coherent. However, I have been highly praised for public speaking while hallucinating, so perhaps it is indeed just a reaction. It is understandable how speaking or organizational skills could easily be compromised when trying to sort out hallucinations or delusions from "shared" reality.

Although most people who experience delusions and hallucinations react to them in the ways defined above, it seems that the definition may be creating another false linkage. It could be that hallucinations and delusions are the only symptoms, and everything else is a reaction to these states. Is it true that the only possible reactions to hallucinations and delusional thoughts are adverse ones? My experience says the answer is no. It seems wrong to link the symptoms and reactions together as if there are no other possible reactions. By calling it a "disorder," hallucinations and delusions are commonly seen entirely in a negative light.

I have a long and rich history of hallucinations and delusional thinking. Since early childhood, I have had so many visions, physical sensations, voices, paranoia, delusions, sounds, feelings, and other experiences that I no longer find them anything but commonplace. For many years, I have been able to tell "shared" reality from "private" reality and even know which "private" ones are common with others, such as breathless states, kundalini energies, seeing the spiritual eye, auras, etc. Although my perspective is that "private" experiences are neither more nor less significant than "shared" experiences, several stand out in the same way that many "shared" life experiences stand out more than others.

One set of "private" experiences is illustrative. I recently visited my mother in the hospital. Convinced that this may be our last chance, my daughter Kate and I flew to visit her after she had been hospitalized for over a month. She had deteriorated to the point that everyone was concerned. Although Kate and I saw many of the same indications, there were a few things that I saw that Kate did not perceive. For example, I witnessed her aura shrinking and her soul receding from her eyes.

A few weeks later, I was walking down Chestnut Street with my wife Ellen when a very common hallucination happened--I jumped in front of an oncoming bus and was killed instantly as I felt my body being crushed. This ordinarily doesn't even phase me any more, but this time it was different. I instantly found myself inside of Ellen and was screaming and shaking from the shock of seeing it happen. Although I am pretty sure I continued to walk down the street without breaking stride, internally I staggered down the street in total shock and could barely hang on to reality.

After about a block I began to tell Ellen about what had happened and we discussed it for several more blocks. I still think about it often. I interpret it to mean that my subconscious mind was helping me process the realization that my mother is not going to live to 100 or so as I have always pretended to be the case. Having managed a retirement home, I watched many people die soon after recovering from an intense illness. My experience tells me that it is better to assume she may not live as long as I had hoped.

My "shock" of seeing my suicide from Ellen's point of view helps me to understand the desperation I sense when I hear the "think about those you will leave behind" argument in conversations about what to say when somebody brings up suicide. Having experienced the suicide point of view, I also understand why it often does not work. For some people it can have the opposite effect. It may remind them how alone they feel. For others, the state is so intense that there are no other people--only the pain.

My ability to hallucinate and think in delusional ways, while having the awareness to realize what is happening, has been a tremendous source of insight for me. I consider it a great gift that I am able to have such experiences. Although they are no more significant than many "real" experiences that I find meaning in, they are also not less significant either.

For those of you who do not hallucinate, imagine having a dream with the same elements as I described. In young children, the response is usually that they want the nightmares to go away. However, many adults feel a sense that we can find meaning in our dreams.

Unlinking Symptoms From Reactions

This false linkage of symptoms to reactions creates a belief that it is not possible to have mental conditions and thrive. It sets up a self-fulfilling prophesy that proves itself by the way that the diagnosed are treated. Since it is believed impossible to thrive in depression, mania, hallucination, and delusion, we are not taught how to, and are instead taught only how to avoid the symptoms and live in fear that they might some day return.

In addition, we are often overmedicated to the point that we cannot possibly work on understanding the condition because our minds are too unclear to think. We end up following the ignorant advice that the only way is to avoid symptoms at all costs, even if the cost is a life not worth living. This linkage is not only wrong, it is tremendously harmful.

We must break the bonds of the false definition and see that it is our inability to react properly to the condition that is the problem. How we define our condition plays an important role in how we perceive it and what steps we take to address it. Separating the reaction from the experience in our definition is an important step toward transforming our condition from a "disorder" to "in order."

Illness vs Condition

The belief that the world was flat kept anyone from sailing far enough West to prove it wrong. In the same way, calling depression, mania, hallucination, and delusion "illnesses" or "disabilities" has the same effect. As long as we cling to the belief that there is nothing good about our condition, we will never make the effort to prove it wrong.

I prefer to call it a "condition" instead of "illness" or "disability." Condition means "the circumstances affecting the way in which people live"[1] and carries no positive or negative connotation. Choosing to see it as a condition opens up the possibility that we can turn it into something positive in our lives.

Just as the false linkage of symptom and reaction in the definition causes great harm, thinking of it as a "disability" creates loss of hope. Although it is clearly disabling for most people who have our condition, it is the labeling as such that keeps us from even trying to make it anything other than something to endure or avoid.

People love to compare mental conditions to physical ones. It seems to create a concreteness to the state as if a mental condition is somehow less valid. Researchers, possibly motivated by the pharmaceutical companies, have gone to great lengths to prove that there is a physical aspect to the

---

1 New Oxford American Dictionary, 2nd Edition

condition. Patients have gladly accepted this view as proof somehow that they have no responsibility for it.

I often read and hear arguments comparing mental conditions to cancer or an amputation. They cite the physical aspects along with the inability to fully function to claim that mental conditions are just as much of a "disability" as the loss of a leg. While this argument sounds good on the surface, it is on par with the flat earth argument once you have seen the other side.

Just like what Columbus was subjected to for challenging the beliefs of his day, I often receive strong arguments accusing me of being dangerous or judgmental for suggesting that there is an element of responsibility in how we react to our condition. A recent comment is illustrative: "Is my mental illness a result of my failure to take control of my life and do things like 'master rage?' If so, is my illness merely a matter of my poor character? Or failure/ unwillingness to change? The danger of such thoughts for me is that they can lead to crushing guilt."

It is so much easier to hold on to the disability argument that many would rather be disabled for the rest of their lives than face the possibility that they may be wrong. Keeping in mind that the "illness" refers to disability, not the condition, the answer is yes. Your mental "illness" is partly a result of your failure to take control of your life and do things like "master rage." We must be careful not to use "illness" as an excuse or justification for our behavior.

Taking responsibility might even bring up feelings of guilt for our past and current actions. Allowing those feelings to be "crushing" is another disabling wrong reaction to a very real "condition." A well developed program as outlined in the *How To Get There* section needs to address those issues also.

The illness vs condition argument applies to psychosis also. The argument was made beautifully in the book *The Natural Mind* by Andrew Weil, MD:

> "Psychotics are persons whose nonordinary experience is exceptionally strong. If they have not integrated this experience into conscious awareness (or so repressed it that it causes physical illness), it takes very negative mental forms. But every psychotic is a potential sage or healer and to the extent that negative psychotics are burdens to society, to that extent can positive psychotics be assets... They possess the secret to changing reality by changing the mind; if they can learn to use that talent for positive ends, there are no limits to what they can accomplish."[1]

I couldn't have said it better myself! His solution: "To effect this transformation we must remove obstacles to the change... and bring patients into contact with healed compatriots--that is, with persons who have themselves made the transformation." That is exactly what this book is about and why peer support should be given only by those who have the condition "in order."

---

1 Weil, Andrew, MD, The Natural Mind, 1972, Houghton Mifflin Company, Boston, p.181

Having seen the other side, I find it as impossible to accept the disability argument as Columbus could agree that the world was flat. I may have been temporarily disabled by my inability to control my reaction, but I certainly am not missing a leg. As I outlined in the *Results Worth Striving For* section, it is an advantage to have our condition once we understand it.

Mood vs Behavior Disorder

Another notion that needs to be challenged is that depression and bipolar are "mood disorders," while hallucinations and delusions are "thought disorders." There is nothing wrong with having moods, thoughts, feelings, visions, delusions, or any other experiences. The problem is our behavior.

Mood is "a conscious state of mind or predominant emotion."[1] Psychology likes to add disclaimers to it like long lasting or long term, but the essential element is not how long it lasts, it is the emotional feeling that we have.

Behavior is "the manner of conducting oneself, anything that an organism does involving action and response to stimulation, and the response of an individual, group, or species to its environment."[2] I would include our thought process as part of the response.

It is interesting that bipolar is called a "mood disorder" but is treated at a behavioral health clinic. If you think about what the "disorder" is for people around a person with depression, mania, hallucination, and delusion, it is the behavior that is the problem. Does it matter if I hallucinate all day long if my behavior does not bother anyone or myself? Does it matter if I am manic or depressed if my actions are completely under self-mastery?

---

1 http://www.merriam-webster.com/dictionary/mood

2 http://www.merriam-webster.com/dictionary/behavior

There is no such thing as disorder of mood. Calling depression and mania "mood disorders" or hallucinations and delusions "thought disorders" is misleading. We should be calling them "behavior disorders."

This line of reasoning is very difficult for people for the same reasons the previous chapters are--it puts the responsibility for the condition where it belongs. The only way to get any of our conditions "in order" is to focus on the behaviors both internal and external. All other efforts are peripheral to this task.

Getting our moods or hallucinations minimized can be an important first step towards getting behavior under control. But, if removal of symptoms is the final goal, then we will never get our condition "in order." The final goal should be having our behavior under self-mastery no matter what moods or other states we are experiencing.

While medicine and the many other therapeutic and self-help approaches may help manage the symptoms, without the goal of behavioral changes they will not get you to an "in order" condition. Treatments may help relieve the symptoms, but leave you with the same behavioral problems that are the bane of the condition. Better to make the primary focus behavioral change while using the other components in the program as aids to assist in the primary goal.

While I agree that for most people there is a point that we lose the ability to choose how to react, I believe we are capable of moving that point far further than we accept. My premise is that once someone gets to a "stable" condition in a range where he/she has the choice of how to respond, we can help expand that range in areas previously outside of it. While I experience states where my own choice is less than optimal, I would never describe it as having little or no choice at all. The more I experience such states with awareness, the more choice I have.

I don't think anyone is advocating living a life so diminished that we live in a zero range of no moods at all; at least not permanently. The important questions are: How wide can the range safely be? What is the best way to get there? Do we try to control the moods or do we try to control the behaviors as defined by the mental and physical reactions to the moods?

My own experience, and that of many others, is that the controllable range is a lot wider than generally believed to be possible. As outlined in the *Perspective* chapter, we are capable of behaving under self-mastery in the full range of moods. This is true at least in those who are willing to do the hard work necessary to achieve it.

There are three main factors influencing our ability to control our behaviors: how far outside of our comfort zone we are, how long we have been there, and what skills we have developed to maintain our behavior. For most, the manic side is much more difficult to control. The extra energy and rapid thoughts make it difficult to maintain composure and have free choice in our reactions. We sometimes need to slow down our reactions so wisdom has a chance to intervene. It is often necessary to reign in our condition in order to maintain self-control.

This is where the original debate about mood vs behavior comes in--I find that if I focus on controlling the moods by trying to not have them, I have no skills to manage my behavior when they do come. When I focus on behavior, the moods become less relevant and I see that mood and behavior are not linked as we have been led to believe. I am in better control of the experience and can function just fine in whatever mood comes my way, while recognizing when it is time to reign in the mood.

Calling it a "mood disorder" makes us focus on trying to control our moods, which minimizes our lives. Focusing on the behaviors allows us to experience the full range that life has to offer without suffering the consequences of our adverse reactions to it. The same logic applies to hallucinations and delusions.

I Am Not A Special Case

I often hear the argument that I am a special case or that my success is because I have such a mild form of bipolar. The implication is that following the advice of this book will not work because it only applies to people with minor conditions or possessing special traits.

As you can read in this and my previous books, my condition is as extreme as most and was once just as "disordered." Just ask anyone who had to deal with me before getting my condition "in order." They have the scars to prove it. It does not mean that I have a minor condition just because I no longer exhibit behaviors as reckless as I once did. The truth is that my condition has gotten much more intense as I learned to function in it, not less. The only thing that has diminished is the power that my condition has in controlling my reaction to it.

It is very common for anyone to think that his/her case is worse than everyone else's. When I was first diagnosed, I read as many books as I could and did not find anyone as bad off as myself. I now understand that my perception was delusional, but it seemed very real at the time. No matter how intense our condition, if we look hard enough we can find someone with similar circumstances, yet functioning with greater self-mastery.

Getting past the belief that our own condition is worse than others or that those who have found success are somehow special is a critical step in the process toward

Bipolar In Order. We need to understand that the "my case is worse" argument is part of the problem. Because that attitude feeds the false belief that improvement is not possible, it will keep us from making any effort at all to better ourselves. We can all achieve clear and measurable results if we develop a realistic plan and make the effort to carry it out.

How To Get There

The journey to the New World did not start with Columbus getting into the dingy and rowing ashore to meet the natives. He had to assemble a team that could accomplish the various tasks, learn the skills needed to succeed, assess the starting point in relation to the goal, plan for the navigation and other steps, and tackle the many problems along the way.

In a similar manner, the journey to *Bipolar In Order* does not begin with equanimity. Change for a person in a suicidal depression does not come from being told to snap out of it, which could make matters worse. In much the same way, letting mania go unchecked is irresponsible and brings with it serious problems. We need to become better educated, create an integrated team, thoroughly assess our current condition, create a Life Plan, and treat the various aspects of our condition.

The most logical process for making any change is to gather together different points of view and do a thorough assessment of the situation before coming up with a plan of action. As with any plan, it is important to lay a foundation and do the steps in order. Once the plan is implemented, it is best to reevaluate on a regular basis and make adjustments as needed. This approach is just as valid for business as it is for an individual.

The Bipolar Advantage approach addresses the whole person with an integrated program led by a professional team. An integrated approach should include the physical, mental, emotional, spiritual, relationship, and career/ financial aspects of life with team members who specialize in the various components.

Central to the Bipolar Advantage approach is acceptance, introspection, mind skills development, creating a Life Plan, and getting help. This section outlines the *Integrated Team Approach, Education, Assessment, Life Planning*, and *Treatment* options that help you to get there. The following section, *Advantage Program Components*, details the role of each element of the integrated team and how they fit together.

All programs need to be individualized based on thorough assessment and planning. For various reasons, including financial as well as geographical location, it is not always possible to create the "ideal" team. One's team may begin with only a therapist or clergy as the support person. The important step to take is to start. By making the effort it is reasonable to expect clear and measurable results within six months.

The optimal results outlined in this book will not happen in six months. It may take several years to begin to fully realize the advantages of our mental conditions. Clear and measurable short term results should give solid indication that the situation is improving and provide proof that the process works. A little success goes a long way toward making the effort and changes necessary to achieve higher goals.

Integrated Team Approach

The most effective way to treat any condition is to approach it from a multifaceted perspective. You can't just adjust one element and expect the entire problem will change. What is needed is an integrated approach that treats the whole person.

Some individuals only take prescription medications and expect them to completely solve their problems. The medicine itself is not the problem. The problem is that we expect medicine alone to do the work without the help of other components of an integrated program.

What we need to do is see all of the approaches as various tools that we can use to solve the problem. Just as a mechanic has pliers, wrenches, jacks, and diagnostic tools, we need to have all of the tools at our disposal so that we can choose the correct one at the appropriate time. Leaving any of the tools out of the toolkit only limits the options and leaves us searching for a tool when we need it the most.

An integrated approach treats the whole individual, including physical, mental, emotional, spiritual, relationships, and career/financial aspects. An integrated team includes experts in all of these disciplines working together for the common goal.

The various disciplines have tremendous overlap and you can often find someone who claims to be expert in many of them. It is important to avoid such practice as it limits the points of view to one person who may not have the ability to see as well as a team can. Experts need to be involved in education, assessment, planning, and treatment as outlined in the following chapters.

The following chart outlines how the various elements fit together into an integrated approach, including how they overlap. Each aspect is detailed in the *Advantage Program Components* section. While each individual is different and may already have some of the areas "in order," it is important to at least consider having someone to consult with in the areas listed. You may choose completely different elements that fit your needs, but should make sure that you are accounting for physical, mental, emotional, spiritual, relationships, and career/financial aspects of life.

	Physical	Mental	Emotional	Spiritual	Relationships	Career/Financial
Peer	*	*	*	*	*	*
Psychiatry		√	√	√	√	*
Psychotherapy		√	√	√	√	*
Relationships		√	√	*	√	√
Mind Skills		√	√	*	*	*
Spiritual		*	√	√	*	
Family & Friends	*	*	*	*	√	*
Addiction	√	√	√	*	√	
Career Coaching					*	√
Financial Coaching					*	√
Physical Therapy	√	√	√	*		
Fitness	√	*	*	*		
Nutrition	√	√	√	*	*	
Medical Doctor	√	√	*	*		
Add Yours						

√ **Directly applies**   * **May apply**

Education

The first step toward mastery of any topic is education. Benefiting from knowledge gained by experts in the field has been a tried and true formula since time immemorial. In this regard, putting bipolar "in order" begins with education.

With the advent of the internet, educational opportunities abound. With them comes a new problem: which ones can be trusted to deliver useful information? While many sources are accurate from a factual standpoint, they more often advocate avoidance rather than developing an understanding of the actual condition.

When I first started going to support groups, I met many people who had encyclopedic knowledge of every drug, dosage, and efficacy. While many people looked up to such displays of memory, I wondered what is the point of memorizing drugs when there are so many other aspects of an integrated approach? If all we focus on are tools to minimize our condition we end up with a diminished life.

It takes careful discrimination to separate the useful sources from those that only create a diminished life. This is a very difficult process that is confounded by the plethora of points of view and the power we give to those who advocate them. While respecting education and experience, it is far more important to look at what results are being proposed. If the outcome is something that you want, consider the steps to success being outlined and determine if it might work for you.

Many professions have a mentor program where the apprentice learns from an accomplished expert. Through books, talks, workshops, videos, and other means, the professional organization builds a knowledge base that helps the students gain proficiency in the field.

The Bipolar Advantage Program is based on the same principles of successful education. By bringing together experts in various disciplines that contribute to a well rounded understanding, we hope to set a new standard for education that leads to *Bipolar In Order*.

This book is the third in the series based on the advantage concepts from a general perspective. Our team members are working on other books from their specific disciplines. We feel that books are an accessible way to disseminate information to a broad audience.

Other means of delivering educational content include websites, videos, magazine articles, and public forums. We have already created materials in these areas and will continue to do so.

The most effective way to learn is in group settings. This is especially important when integrating new ideas that challenge our existing beliefs. Sharing ideas with each other helps us to sort out our own feelings with input from several sources. Professionally facilitated by someone who knows how to keep the conversation on track, we learn more from each other than we can from hearing only one point of view.

In our workshops, lectures are replaced with guided discussions, brainstorming, games, and other activities. Physical and mental exercises, visualizations, meditations, and more are all woven into an experience that will increase learning, memory retention, and practice of useful skills.

Although each of our workshops can be taken separately, the complete series provides a necessary base of knowledge as well as a shift in thinking that leads to success. The Advantage Program workshop series is primarily for those who experience mental health conditions. Family, friends, and professionals are also encouraged to attend. Workshops are designed to be an intensive, interactive environment that encourages participation.

Bipolar In Order Workshop

Facilitated by Tom Wootton

The Bipolar In Order Workshop introduces the central concepts of the Advantage Program while creating the important paradigm shift in thinking. Changing our beliefs from illness based diminished lives to conditions that have both good and bad aspects is the first step toward changing our lives. We will be stuck in the old paradigm of living in fear that we may relapse at any time until we accept the possibility that we can overcome all of our obstacles and create a fabulous life with our condition.

The central concepts are Acceptance, Introspection, Mind Skills Development, Life Planning, and Getting Help. Defining *Results Worth Striving For* and the steps to get there are presented as a clear and logical path. Each of these topics are covered in detail and the participants end the workshop with a clear understanding of what it takes to create a life worth striving for. Through accepting our circumstances and resolving to do something about them, we can enjoy far richer and fulfilling experiences in our lives.

Bipolar In Order Workshop topics:

- A clear and meaningful understanding of the bipolar condition.
- The importance of acceptance in resolving to create a better life.
- Expanding awareness of your thoughts and actions.
- The power of Introspection.
- Habits - how they work and the power to change them.
- Mind Skills - exercises that increase our mental acumen.
- Relationships - understanding how relationships work and how to apply that understanding in your own life.
- Identifying *Results Worth Striving For.*
- Setting goals for physical, mental, emotional, spiritual, relationships, and career/financial aspects of life.
- How to create a Life Plan for success.
- Understanding fears, roadblocks to success, and how to deal with mistakes.
- Getting Help - the importance of an integrated team of support.

This workshop is the foundation of the Advantage Program series. It provides an introduction to the other workshops and a clear understanding of the Bipolar Advantage main concepts.

Mind Skills Training

Facilitated by Brian Weller

Managing the mind is an essential step to gain greater control in life, especially for those with a bipolar condition. A critical key in changing our responses is to change the way we see or interpret situations. What we tell ourselves when we experience any condition either moves us toward or away from a more optimum state of being.

Our thinking and our relationship with ourselves is where we have the greatest potential for breakthroughs. During the Mind Skills training, students learn how to see the mindsets, belief systems, and frames of reference that are operating in their lives and how to develop new ways of thinking.

Managing stress is also an essential part of the training. Some of the finest approaches to both understanding and mastering the stress response are presented. Do we simply react to what happens, or can we learn to use stress breaking techniques and strategies to go beyond our habits and become masters of our experience?

Students learn focusing techniques and how to settle the mind into states of ease and calm. By relaxing the mind and releasing tension, we can become more aware of subtler levels of thinking and more conscious of what is happening, both in the world around us and in ourselves. We teach how to get more in touch with inner knowing, how to use this to open up to deeper feelings, and better manage emotions.

An important part of the program covers Mindmapping, the master note taking skill that develops memory, attention, and creativity in order to be more effective in daily tasks. Mindmapping helps enable students to create Life Plans, be more creative with brainstorming, explore ideas with friends and family, and generally enhance careers.

Memory training is a featured part of Mind Skills. Improving memory for different types of information with short and long term recall builds confidence. We all have vast, untapped mental potential and releasing this in practical ways is both life-affirming as well as useful in the everyday world.

The Mind Skills workshop is designed around core principles based on well established mind/brain research. The style of the training is fun and highly interactive with lots of practice in the skills, including work individually and in small groups. As an integral part of the Bipolar Advantage Program, the Mind Skills workshop integrates and enhances much of the information from the other educational workshops.

Nourishing Relationships That Work

Facilitated by Maureen Duffy, PhD

For better or for worse, relationships influence our overall personal well-being, our health, our jobs and careers, our finances, our view of ourselves, and our feelings about the future. When our relationships are going well, our lives are significantly better than when our relationships are troubled. We all want to have close and satisfying relationships with our friends and family members. Yet, for many people, the work of developing and maintaining positive relationships requires skills that they have never learned or can't quite put into practice in spite of a strong desire to do so.

Nourishing Relationships That Work is a professional relationship training program that will give students the skills and support to bridge the gap between wanting better relationships and actually having them. The program focuses on relationship assessment, relationship goal setting, and on an ongoing process of reflection and action (praxis) needed to achieve desired relationship goals.

In this workshop, students learn how managing themselves and their own emotional responses are key parts of positive relationship building. Understanding and managing our own emotional responses happens when bipolar is "in order." Nourishing Relationships That Work helps us to get there.

Disruptions in relationships are inevitable and there is no such thing as a "perfect" relationship, but "good enough" relationships are essential for keeping bipolar "in order." Developing positive relationships requires us to know how to ask for what we need, to have the humility to accept caring from another, and to consistently act in ways that demonstrate honoring and valuing of human relationships.

Nourishing Relationships That Work topics:

- Stop blaming yourself and other family members for family problems.
- Stop feeling guilty, ashamed, or stigmatized.
- Increase the quality of communication within your family and friends.
- Learn how to successfully handle intense emotion in relationships.
- Develop highly effective non-blaming conflict resolution skills.
- Learn how to develop an appreciative perspective and be in the relationships that you have always wanted to have.
- Strengthen and deepen the bonds of connection within your family and friends.
- Create relationships in which you can turn to each other for support, caring, and love.
- Become a hope-filled family that experiences life deeply while recognizing and celebrating the uniqueness of each family member.

Biopsychosocial Workshop

Facilitated by Dr. Peter Forster, MD

More than 30 years ago, the internist George Engel wrote an article in "Science"[1] calling for a new approach to health. He spoke of developing a biopsychosocial model which recognizes that biological, psychological (for example, thoughts, emotions, and behaviors), and social factors (ab-

---

1 Engel, G. L. (1977, April 8). The need for a new medical model: A challenge for biomedicine. Science, 196, 129-136.

breviated "BPS") all play a critical role in how people deal with or adapt to disease or illness. This is in contrast to the traditional biomedical model of medicine that suggests every disease process can be explained by simple physical events (such as an infectious agent entering the body).

In an article in 2004 reviewing George Engel's legacy, Francesc Borrell-Carrió, et al, wrote: "The biopsychosocial model is both a philosophy of clinical care and a practical clinical guide. Philosophically, it is a way of understanding how suffering, disease, and illness are affected by multiple levels of organization, from the societal to the molecular. At the practical level, it is a way of understanding the patient's subjective experience as an essential contributor to accurate diagnosis, health outcomes, and humane care."[1]

In the Biopsychosocial workshop we identify key biological, psychological and social issues that affect people with mood disorders. Topics include:

- Brain and Mood - We summarize the literature that shows how mood and mood disorders relate to brain functioning. We also present some interesting data that shows that the simplistic notion of "biological" or "non-biological" depression (which somehow predicts whether to treat with medications or psychotherapy) is contradicted by data that shows that psychotherapy works by changing the brain.
- Mood charting, how and why to do it - In this section we discuss why it is important to keep track of mood on a regular basis, why it is often difficult to remem-

---

1 Epstein, Ronald M.,Borrell-Carrio, Francesc, *The biopsychosocial model: exploring six impossible things.* Publication: Families, Systems & Health December 2005

ber how we were feeling later, and what some of the barriers are to paying attention to mood in a constructive way.

○ Social rhythms and the importance of routine - One of the most effective treatments for people with bipolar disorder involves systematically examining and modifying daily social rhythms. Many people with mood disorders find that their lives fall into patterns that may not be that healthy, with too much isolation and too little exposure to the outdoors. We explore how to make changes in this area.

○ Circadian rhythms, light, and sleep - In this portion of the workshop we expand on the topic of our body's "clock" and how it can easily malfunction in our technological society. This malfunction can play a critical role in the development of depression, mania, hallucination, and delusion.

○ Dealing with stress and mindfulness - Most of us "filter" our experience through the lens of thoughts, ideas, fears, beliefs about the world, and our place in it. Often these beliefs lead to unhappiness. We explore how a practice of mindfulness can lead to a clearer sense of the world and a feeling of strength and peace in the face of stress.

○ Interpersonal issues and patterns - Moods and mood disorders have a big impact on relationships. Those who are close to us adapt to how changing moods affect them in ways that may or may not be healthy. Here we examine some common patterns in relationships.

○ Approaches to anxiety - Anxiety often accompanies a mood disorder. In this portion of the workshop we highlight ways of dealing with anxiety, especially approaches that don't involve using medications, such as cognitive and behavioral interventions.

◇ Substances, use and misuse. - Half of those who have mood disorders also have trouble at times with substance use. We explain why this is true and what can be done about it.

◇ Medications - What they can and what they can't do. When dealing with something as nebulous as depression, mania, hallucination, and delusion, it is easy to feel frustrated and to hope that a doctor can find the "perfect" medication regimen that will take away all of our problems. In fact, some people come to see doctors hoping that they can figure out the perfect treatment without having to talk with them, sort of like taking your car in to the mechanic and leaving it there to be fixed.

◇ The value of psychotherapy - We summarize the literature on the effectiveness of psychotherapy for people with mood disorders. We also talk about how enduring patterns can develop in how we perceive the world around us (schemas) and how these patterns may relate to chronic depression.

◇ Diet and health issues - What we eat matters more for those with depression, mania, hallucination, and delusion than those without. People with mental conditions often have nutritional deficiencies, weight problems, diabetes, and a host of other problems related to diet.

Spirituality Workshop

Facilitated by Scott Sullender, PhD

Spirituality in the context of *Bipolar in Order* is defined as:

> *...that aspect of ourselves that seeks to connect us with a transcendental reality that gives our lives ultimate meaning and purpose. We celebrate these ultimate meanings in rituals, myths, and values, and we act out these meanings in moral, ethical, and symbolic behaviors in the world.*

Spirituality is not the same as religion. Spirituality is universal. Everyone has some sense of spirituality, either developed or underdeveloped. Religion is the attempt by groups of people who think about ultimate meanings to organize, structure, define, and thereby limit, their experiences of spirituality. We may or may not ascribe to an organized religion.

Spirituality is highly individualistic. Each of us is on a unique spiritual journey. We are not here to tell you what you ought to do or believe, but to help you explore some spiritual resources that you might use to better enable you to deal with your depression and bipolar conditions.

There are no experts in the realm of spirituality. Spiritual wisdom is found in a variety of faith traditions. In this workshop we try to honor the diversity of various spiritual traditions.

We will do two things in this workshop. First, we will discuss various spiritual principles and how these principles might be applied to your struggle with depression in ways that would enable you to transcend your "disorder."

Secondly, we will introduce various spiritual practices or behaviors that, if practiced regularly, would help you build up the habits, attitudes, and inner strengths you need to combat depression. Some of the topics or issues we will discuss will include:

- Finding meaning in your depression.
- Finding a purpose for your life beyond your condition.
- What is a spiritual crisis?
- Empowering you to forgive yourself and others.
- Use of meditation and contemplative prayer practices.
- Spirituality vs. delusions and hallucinations.
- The life giving attitude of gratitude.
- Developing serenity in an age of desires.
- Sustaining inner peace during depression.

Addictions Workshop

Facilitated by Michael R. Edelstein, PhD

This workshop presents the Rational Emotive Behavior Therapy (REBT) approach for overcoming practical, emotional, and behavioral aspects of addictions. An addiction is defined as any repetitive behavior which interferes with, blocks, or sabotages long-term goals. Addictive behaviors progress from initially harmless, pleasurable activities, to compulsive, driven behaviors that are self-destructive to emotions and life.

REBT posits that addictions are not caused by a dysfunctional childhood, disease, addicted friends or partners, or even by strong cravings for a substance. Rather, they're caused by unrealistic thoughts, beliefs, and attitudes in the present. REBT helps identify addictive thinking and offers a cognitive-behavioral alternative to the 12-step model.

Issues discussed include:

◇ Moderation vs abstinence
◇ Tapering vs cold turkey
◇ The self-esteem trap
◇ The roles played by disease, environment, and genetics in addiction
◇ 12-steps and powerlessness
◇ Avoiding relapse
◇ Secondary disturbance

Participants learn to:

◇ Clearly identify those behaviors which are addictions and those which are not.
◇ Set realistic goals in harnessing addictions.
◇ Identify the irrational beliefs causing addiction problems.
◇ Master cognitive concepts and strategies for overcoming addictive thinking.
◇ Master behavioral tools for overcoming addictions.

Life Planning Workshop

Facilitated by Tom Wootton

This workshop is about creating a plan for our future. Each participant leaves the workshop with a written two year plan that includes Physical, Mental, Emotional, Spiritual, Relationship, and Career/Financial goals. The plans are individualized with clear steps on how to achieve the goals. The Life Plan is the basis for getting life "in order."

By working together to explore both possibilities and steps to achieve realistic goals, the participants learn from each other while writing their own individual plan. The plans are as personal and private as desired, while having the benefit of ideas brainstormed by the entire group. This helps us to not only see what is possible, but to get feedback about the reasonable steps to accomplish the final goals.

The Life Plans are very detailed. Starting with long term dreams, the milestones along the way are clearly spelled out so that we can make our dreams become reality. The end result is a carefully written plan that runs from concrete actions to take on day one, to measurable milestones for one month, three months, six months, one year, and two years.

The Life Plan is further refined and adjusted with guidance from the assessment and treatment team. In the assessment process (outlined in the next chapter), the Life Plan is refined to create clear and achievable steps. In the treatment phase (outlined later), support and insight is provided to help overcome the obstacles that stand in our way.

Bipolar In Order is about defining the life each person feels is worth striving for and having the support and resources to make it happen. Further details are in the *Life Planning* chapter later in the book.

Assessment

Before you can create a plan that will take you to where you want to go, you have to know where you are now. Whether the plan is for a trip to San Francisco or to *Bipolar In Order*, you don't know what path to take or what direction to travel without knowing your starting point. Along the way, you may find yourself off track, so it is equally important to periodically reassess where you are and make adjustments as necessary.

The practice of a fifteen minute assessment and a prescription needs to be relegated to the history books along with drowning women to see if they are witches. You cannot determine in fifteen minutes where you are psychologically any better than finding your location by spinning a globe and poking it with your finger.

It takes a thorough assessment to determine the starting point for getting any mental condition "in order." Thorough means both a deep and wide look at the whole person from several points of view. It is important to examine the physical, mental, emotional, spiritual, relationship, and career/financial aspects to get a complete perspective. Each assessment should be at least one hour and the psychiatrist should optimally spend three hours or more before suggesting treatment approaches.

Communication between all of the assessment team members is a critical part of any thorough approach. Having assessments from many points of view may be substantially better than a single approach, but without sharing the insights they could lead to conflicting conclusions.

Our approach is to use a database that is accessible to all team members; including the client, family, and all of the experts involved. We also have group meetings with the entire team. While the database needs to be HIPAA[1] compliant, the most crucial element is that the client needs to legally approve the information sharing between team members.

The process is to meet with the various team members individually and then assemble the team so that they can share their unique perspectives. For example, the psychiatrist may suggest the need to start a jogging program, but the medical or fitness evaluation might have determined that jogging is not the best approach and suggest swimming instead.

The first use of the thorough assessment is help in creating the Life Plan as detailed in the next chapter. Based on knowing where the client is currently and what the client desires to accomplish, the Life Plan is a critical part of the overall strategy.

Assessments are not a static process. Every time a team member meets with a client for treatment, they are doing an assessment and taking notes about the current conditions. The notes are shared with all team members, including the client. The client's own introspection is a form of assess-

---

1 http://www.hhs.gov/ocr/privacy/hipaa/understanding/index.html
The Privacy Rule provides federal protections for personal health information held by covered entities and gives patients an array of rights with respect to that information. At the same time, the Privacy Rule is balanced so that it permits the disclosure of personal health information needed for patient care and other important purposes.

ment also. The client even has the opportunity to comment and self-assess as part of the database.

The Life Plan includes clear and measurable milestones toward achieving our goals. It is important for the team to reassess the client's condition at each of the milestone dates and make adjustments to the plan. The reassessments are more formal than the ongoing assessments that happen at each meeting. They are geared toward setting the current point of progress and are used as the starting point for changes in the Life Plan as well as treatment regimens.

The assessment process is an integral part of a successful program. It is used as the reference point in developing the Life Plan as well as for making periodic scheduled adjustments. Ongoing assessments are a crucial component in getting any mental condition "in order."

Details of how assessments are done from each point of view are included in the next section - *Advantage Program Components*. While not everyone has the resources or inclination to have such a thorough assessment, this book is about what is ultimately possible. Just as not everyone is interested in achieving equanimity or even the highest level of self-mastery, the assessment should be commensurate with the intended outcomes.

Life Planning

Bipolar In Order is about realizing that it is possible to have *Results Worth Striving For* and doing the work needed to achieve them. Life planning is where the two come together.

A Life Plan should be integrated, clear and measurable, include time based milestones, and be adjusted as needed every few months. This chapter details the process for building a Life Plan and making it succeed. There are many ways to create a Life Plan. Among the many offered, the process outlined here works best for the people that have taken our workshops.

Integrated

An integrated approach addresses the physical, mental, emotional, spiritual, relationship, and career/financial aspects of life. It is important to consider balance as a key to success. If you are doing great in your career, but your relationships are in disrepair, this will have an effect on your mental and emotional life. Any part of your life that is not brought into balance with the others can eventually bring down the rest.

Clear And Measurable

One of the keys to any plan is to have clear and measurable goals. If your goal is not clear and measurable, you will not be able to tell if you've achieved it. A physical goal that says "I will feel better" is so vague that you will never know if you succeeded. A goal that says "I will run 5 miles" is a measurable goal. A goal that says "I will run 5 miles in under 30 minutes within six months" is even more clear. We need to make our goals as clear as possible.

Setting goals for freedom, stability, and equanimity are more difficult to describe. It is important to discuss with your team what success means to you and how you will know when you have accomplished it.

Time Based Milestones

Milestones are a critical part of any plan. In a plan to drive from New York to San Francisco, the milestones might be Cleveland on the first night, Omaha on the second, Denver on the third, Salt Lake City on the fourth, and arrive in San Francisco on the fifth day. If you find yourself in Washington, DC on the first night, you better change the route and call ahead to tell them you will be there on the sixth day!

A plan for getting life in order is far more complex, but the main principle is the same: create achievable milestones, periodically check to see where you are, and make changes as necessary.

As the trip from "disorder" to "in order" is much longer than New York to San Francisco, it is necessary to follow a much longer time frame. Reasonable milestones should be established for one day, one month, three months, six months, one year, and two years. Five and ten year goals are even reasonable, but as you follow the plan, you may find that the original goals are no longer important to you.

You might even create a new plan with different short and long-term goals after the first two years.

Milestones should always be based on a reasonable time frame to achieve them. If we don't set a timeframe, we may never finish. On the other hand, if we set timeframes that are too short, we may feel a sense of defeat and give up on achieving our goals.

As a brief example, let's say you want to run a marathon (26.2 miles) two years from today. In order to know that you are on track, you should be able to run at least 10 miles one year from today. A reasonable goal for six months would be 5 miles. You should be running 2 miles in three months, 1 mile within one month, and perhaps start out by walking a mile on the first day. Milestones are clear and measurable results that indicate whether you are on track to achieving your long term goals.

Creating A Vision

The first step to writing a plan is visualizing what you want your life to be. This is the Grand Vision phase-- imagining the ultimate dream life. At this point you assume that you can accomplish anything that you want. If you don't imagine that you are capable of your dreams, you will not set very high goals. Keep in mind the *Results Worth Striving For* section. Our vision needs to be worth making the effort to achieve it.

Many people say that those who create a clear vision are the most likely to achieve it. Visualization is a powerful technique for seeing all of the details and creating the motivation to take the steps needed to turn the vision into a reality. Those of us that hallucinate have a gift that we can turn to our advantage. We can use that gift to create a picture of our future and even see the steps to get there.

Capture the vision by writing down everything in as much detail as possible. Focus on your surroundings, the way that you feel, the people involved, and any specifics that you notice. Record all that you envision and try not to leave anything out, even if it may seem insignificant at the time.

Expect to spend two hours or more on this process. It takes that long as a directed exercise in our workshops. We have forms from the workshops available on our web site that might be a helpful template.[1]

Determine Strengths And Weaknesses

Assessment gives an understanding of where you are. Now that you have a vision, it is time to put the assessment into context. In looking at the vision, write down what strengths will help you achieve them and what weaknesses need to be overcome.

You will have some obvious strengths and weaknesses in each area of your life. When you write down your weaknesses, you may be surprised to learn that others don't view those traits as weaknesses. Some traits that you consider a weakness might be turned to your advantage. It is important to look at the list with the team and determine if

1 www.bipolarinorder.com

there are things you are simply afraid to do, or don't have confidence you can do. Team members will perceive strengths that you either discount or didn't realize you had.

This process will give you a better understanding of what needs to be done to accomplish your goals. Working through it carefully is time well spent.

Set Milestones

Now, you can begin to be more pragmatic and analytical about the visions you have created. Some goals might be 20 or 30 year goals. What do you think you can achieve in two years? These are the things you want to write into your Life Plan.

Organize the Life Plan by taking a separate page for each area of focus: Physical, Mental, Emotional, Spiritual, Relationships, and Career/Financial. Bipolar Advantage uses a worksheet that has room for 1 day, 1 month, 3 months, six months, 1 year, and 2 years as the timeline for milestones. It is available on our website.[1]

Using physical goals as an example, you should consider strength, flexibility, body awareness, weight, endurance, and appearance. Milestones should be set with clear interim steps toward achieving each goal.

The same process is used for mental, emotional, spiritual, relationship, and career/financial goals. Always be careful that the goals are reasonable and easy to achieve. Go

---

1 www.bipolarinorder.com

over the plan with your team and make sure you can meet these goals.

The next step is combining all the goals onto one sheet. When seen together in one place, what you thought was very easy may suddenly look impossible. Make sure you haven't created an overwhelming task. If so, you may have to be more realistic about some of the timelines. The other thing to consider is whether the plan is in balance. Is there too much emphasis on only one part of your life?

Do not underestimate the power of the process of writing the plan. Becoming clear about where you want to go is very liberating and exciting. We have seen people write a complete plan, throw it in a drawer and never look at it again, yet still achieve most of their goals.

Do The Work

Having a plan is only as good as our efforts to carry it out. You will need to do the hard work necessary to make it happen and be willing to adapt the plan according to your circumstances. Every day you should make an effort to accomplish the short term goals that you have set out for yourself.

Adjusting The Plan

If you have only arrived at your three month goal after six months, that's a tremendous victory--aren't you still better off than if you had not made any effort? Simply adjust your timetables and keep moving forward. At each milestone date, evaluate the progress with your team and make adjustments to the plan as needed to keep on track for the goals. Periodic adjustments are the difference between success and failure in all endeavors. They are not a sign of failure, but a sign of wisdom gained through experience.

Treatment

Left untreated, depression and bipolar can rapidly escalate through disorder to illness and even death. It is the height of foolishness to allow the symptoms to go unchecked. Treating the condition can literally mean the difference between life and death.

The most common treatments available today are medication and psychotherapy. Unfortunately, over reliance on medicines to suppress the symptoms often leads to a life not worth living. Abuses of both medicine and psychotherapy have led to discouraged and demoralized patients. Limiting treatment to only two approaches is not working for too many people. We need a complete set of tools that can be combined in ways that are both effective and attractive to the client if we are to succeed.

Current approaches are positive because they are beginning to recognize the power of bringing different disciplines into equal participation. It is well established that cognitive therapy[1] and/or family focused therapy[2] along with judicial use of medication can create lasting benefit for those who have lost control of their condition. Similarly, studies have shown that it is most effective to treat addictions and bipolar or depressive conditions on a parallel

---

1 "Psychotherapies", Mental Health Topics, The National Institute of Mental Health, http://www.nimh.nih.gov/health/topics/psychotherapies/index.shtml

2 Ibid

program.[1] The combination can be an important first step on a path to *Bipolar In Order* and can help patients get to a stable condition of dramatically reduced symptoms. The problem lies in thinking that reduction of symptoms is the end goal of treatment. Just as mental conditions can progress from disorder to illness and death, we must change the treatment goals to progress from "symptom free" to *Bipolar In Order*. A well designed treatment approach should have *Results Worth Striving For* as the end goal.

The Bipolar Advantage program builds on current approaches by adding more elements to the treatment. Our approach incorporates peer coaching, psychiatry, psychotherapy, medication, relationship counseling, mind skills coaching, spiritual counseling, family & friends, addictions counseling, career management counseling, financial coaching, physical rehabilitation therapy, nutrition counseling, fitness coaching, primary care physician, and more as directed by the client.

Real success depends on treating the whole person including physical, mental, emotional, spiritual, relationships, and career/financial aspects. A truly integrated system is not just across disciplines. It brings each aspect into participation across all phases of the program: *Education, Assessment, Life Planning,* and *Treatment.*

Continuing the integrated approach throughout treatment enables the client to succeed in all areas of life. It insures confidence by minimizing failures that impede progress and by increasing the areas of success that contribute

---

1 Forster, Peter, MD and Tierney, Matt, RN, CNS, NP, "Substance Abuse in Patients with Depression and Anxiety", January 2006, San Francisco Medicine- the journal of the San Francisco Medical Society

to the overall sense of well being. Progress helps clients to continue with the effort and reinforces the idea that they can and will succeed.

Because the Bipolar Advantage program is focused on a holistic integration of multiple elements, treatment delivery is provided in a variety of ways. Options include traditional face to face contact, phone, internet, support groups, and full team meetings.

The Bipolar Advantage treatment approach is based on the Life Plan. As the Life Plan has very high, yet reasonable, expectations, the program is designed to give the support necessary to achieve major changes and set the foundation for a lifetime of growth. The specific methods chosen should be dependent on the current condition and desired outcomes. Any treatment program needs to be individually tailored to the specific needs and resources available. An integrated team is individually customized and includes family, friends, and other providers as approved and controlled by the client.

Treatment approaches for specific components in the program are detailed in the *Advantage Program Components* section. You can use it as a guide to developing your own treatment program.

Advantage Program Components

The Advantage Program came together through a series of discussions and dialogs with members of our Advantage Program Team. We designed each component to address specific needs and to work in cooperation with the others. The contributing authors have written what they hope will become a model for integrated care, including why their component is an important part of it. Each chapter describes their contribution to assessment and treatment while working cooperatively with each other.

This section of the book can serve as a guide in putting your team together. It will provide a basic understanding of how each professional contributes to wellness and how they might interact with the other members of your team. Some of these services will not be covered by insurance or fall under one office or clinic. Creatively assembling an integrated team and following the model will be worth the effort.

For mental health professionals, we hope this section will provide a model program to establish integrated care for the clients you serve. Again, while it is tempting to site that one's own professional offerings include guidance on a number of topics listed here, it is more important to offer the client a variety of viewpoints and expertise from different sources that are cooperative and complimentary to the others.

The following chapters provide an outline of what the components are and how they contribute to the overall program. Written by actual team members, the descriptions follow a common pattern. *Point of View* describes the unique perspective that the practitioner of that component provides. *Integration With Team* covers how the component fits in with the rest of the program. *Assessment Process* looks at the logistics of how assessments are made. *Goal Setting* discusses how this component helps in creating the Life Plan. Finally, *Treatment* outlines specific treatment protocols for that component.

There are many other components that exist which could help individuals with specific needs and backgrounds. Your individual plan may include additional components not listed here. All components lead toward the final goal of having *Bipolar In Order*.

Peer Coaching

Point Of View

Peer support is a critical part of the path to *Results Worth Striving For*. We see ourselves as advocates who have direct experience of navigating the path to success. We have the ultimate form of empathy, knowing the condition from both sides: "disorder" and "in order." Having successfully completed the Advantage Program, we are familiar with the processes and points of view of the whole team. A well trained peer can be the important difference between success and a diminished life.

Integration With Team

The peer is the advocate for the client and the translator for the rest of the team members. The client may not fully agree with assessments or treatments advocated by the other team members, but have a hard time communicating such perceptions or issues. Since peers share the client's point of view and also communicate regularly with the other team members, we are in a unique position to speak effectively with both parties. The peer is a critical resource for all involved and is the tie that binds them together.

Assessment Process

The assessment that a peer supporter provides is invaluable to the entire team. It is easier for us to establish trust and empathy because we know what questions to ask and, because of our experiences, can better determine the accuracy of answers. Clients freely admit that they lie to their therapists and families, but tend to be more open with a peer. There is a greater feeling of trust when talking with someone that you know has had the same or similar experiences. As they say, "It takes one to know one!"

The assessment is done via one or more one-to-one interviews that are guided more by establishing rapport than by a fixed set of questions. It is more important to establish open communication than to get a specific result.

The peer assessment brings insights to the team that do not turn up in the other assessments. While psychological and other evaluations focus on specific diagnostic criteria, our focus is on assessing the client's potential strengths. We alleviate the client's fears about the process while helping him/her to see the value in staying with the entire program.

Goal Setting

Peer coaches ensure the goals set by the other team members are reasonable and within the limitations of the current state of the client. At the same time, the unique perspective the peer has from interactions with the client allows the peer to know if the goals are stimulating, engaging, and what the client really wants. Overall, the peer coach balances challenging long term goals with feasible short term goals. The peer knows what the effort feels like firsthand and can inform the whole team about the difficulties at all stages of the process.

Goal setting for the peer is the fun part. The peer is advocating for an extraordinary life that is worth striving for. We have the opportunity to encourage the family and friends on the team that there is hope and that the path outlined can be achieved. They need to see someone who is an example of what their loved one can become and we get to be that example of hope. It is a very rewarding part of the process.

While other team members are specific in their goals, the peer goals are global. Our involvement in the planning process is not specific to any one area. We talk more about breakthroughs and realizations than the more defined milestones like jogging distance or sit-ups completed. The other experts on the team cover the details; we look at the big picture and make sure the sum of the parts does not add up to an overwhelming program.

Treatment

Peers support the client so that they can achieve the goals the client and team members have outlined in the Life Plan. Our role in the treatment phase is accomplished through one-to-one coaching and support groups. One-to-one coaching focuses on individual issues in a private setting. Support groups are meetings with others who share similar goals that are directed by a trained peer facilitator.

One-to-one coaching is not therapy. Issues around medication or topics that are better handled by the other experts are deferred to the appropriate resource. The peer's role is to be the one with empathy that can encourage the client to keep on the path to success. This does not mean that the peer role is somehow less important. To the contrary, the peer is the only one who has been down the path and can recognize where the client is veering off. The peer brings insight to the entire team while being the main cheerleader that keeps the client making the effort.

We meet regularly in person, via phone, or internet to discuss areas in which the client might be struggling. From our unique perspective we are able to offer guidance. If a client has issues or concerns about their treatment program, we work with them on how to improve the program for their individual needs. These discussions enable us to provide valuable feedback to the other team members to make the client's experience even more worthwhile.

Our support groups are topic-based. In a sense they are like mini workshops. Each meeting covers a specific topic in depth and ends with homework to prepare for the next meeting. Support group facilitation takes great skill to be effective. It takes training and experience to keep the conversation on track while getting all participants fully engaged. Being able to "feel the energy" of the group and know when to change activities is more art than science. We use a combination of directed conversations with the whole group, small group discussions in groups of three or four, and individual introspection, all interwoven with lecture, videos, games, and other teaching methods.

The power of well facilitated group work is that it reinforces strength-based learning. The focus is on progress and personal growth. Each person brings different insight that contributes to the understanding and education of others. It also creates important bonds that work outside the group to help each other stay on track. Participants often comment that it is good to know they are not alone. They develop friendships and have a new sense of belonging and hope.

In the support group environment, not only do we have the leader exhibiting a high level of success, but others in the group are examples of the process at different stages of development. This helps all participants see what can be accomplished in the short- as well as long-term. It also lets members see others on the path to success and this builds confidence in their own efforts.

It is important to differentiate between peer support by someone coming from success and what is practiced all too often in the peer support community. If the peer does not have the condition "in order" and is failing in his/her own life, how can the support lead to anything but a similar failure? Walking someone down a path that did not work out will only confuse him/her and strengthen the false belief that we need to accept failure as the outcome.

Many doctors hesitate to send patients to peer support organizations because they see the shortcomings of the approach when done wrong. We have developed a support group model that promises genuine learning and better outcomes.

The most important outcomes of our peer program are having graduates who are examples of success that people can aspire to. Successful peers encourage a responsible approach to improving our lives.

Psychiatry

Peter Forster, MD

Point Of View

As physicians, psychiatrists begin with a perspective that has been called "the medical model." There are many definitions of this term; mine is "the predominant Western approach to illness, the body being a complex mechanism, with illness understood in terms of causation and remediation, in contrast to holistic and social models." One key aspect of the model is the notion of diagnosis. The psychiatrist identifies conditions, known as disorders, that are felt to underlie difficulties that the patient is experiencing in daily life.[1]

The disease model represented a significant advance in the approach to people with depression and bipolar as contrasted to models that were common in the late 19th century. The close connection between a disease model, which is often associated with biological explanations, and reductions in stigma has been noted by many. In fact, advocates for those with bipolar and depression generally favor a disease model as contrasted with other models which, for instance, might result with having people who are manic incarcerated as opposed to treated.

---

1 Diagnostic and Statistical Manual of Mental Disorders, Fourth Edition (American Psychiatric Association, 1994

Modern imaging techniques have pointed to changes in both structure and function of the brain. It is now clear that similar kinds of brain changes take place when people are treated with medications, or with psychotherapy. Most psychiatrists don't view psychiatric disorders as either biological or psychological, but instead tend to view these conditions as having psychological, biological, social, and spiritual dimensions.

"Does it work" is the question psychiatrists focus on. This pragmatic approach can be frustrating in that it may make people feel as if they're simply undergoing a series of experiments. At best, it reflects a willingness to try a varied approach as outlined in this book. At the same time, it demonstrates a willingness to change what is done based on new clinical research.

Integration With Team

Psychiatry is often defined by the effectiveness of its collaborative skills. One of the trademark features of the Bipolar Advantage Program is the commitment that team members have to work with each other. In out-patient settings, most people practice on their own and have a set of other practitioners that they often collaborate with. It is beneficial to have a psychiatrist and a therapist who have worked together successfully in the past. This way, communication is far simpler. Occasionally, it may be important to schedule a team meeting for the different providers to share opinions with each other.

This type of integration doesn't happen as often as it should. In part because it isn't covered by insurance and because most health care professionals, both mental and physical, are more comfortable with an individual practice model. The integrated approach outlined in this book challenges the status quo by taking integration to the next level.

Assessment Process

Much of psychiatric assessment is based on a very careful and methodical history-gathering process. The goal in the assessments of those with depression and bipolar is to have a clear sense of several things: how people's symptoms have changed over time, the transitional process from one mood state to another, how quickly those transitions take place, and if there were any patterns that can be recognized. Information regarding any influence treatment has had on the course of symptoms is also noted. This very careful and thoughtful analysis not only takes time, but also requires a fair amount of help from the patient.

Another part of the psychiatric evaluation is the mental status examination. This is a structured way of evaluating the important dimensions of mental functioning: mood, attention, memory, patterns of thinking, et cetera. The psychiatrist compares what he finds through the mental status examination with information that he has about typical patterns of thought and emotions found in different conditions. The psychiatrist may request psychological tests to more precisely define the nature of the psychological processes. The psychiatrist may well order some screening laboratory studies, and perhaps neuroimaging, electrocardiogram, or electroencephalogram (EEG).

All of this information is used to identify a diagnosis from which the psychiatrist is able to make suggestions for treatment. The recommendations are based on scientific literature which looks at how others with similar problems respond to treatment.

The focus leans toward symptoms and diagnosis, more so than functioning, although both are important. It's a frequent criticism of psychiatric assessment that psychiatrists focus more on problems than on creative adaptation. People are not just a sum of their problems, they also have come up with creative solutions to these problems. For instance, one person with a severe depression may be unable to leave their bed, whereas another person may have found a way to continue to function normally.

One thing that is important is to find a way of keeping track of mood states and transitions. This is especially true because of a phenomenon called State Dependent Learning. This phenomenon is based on how the brain stores memory. The hippocampus, which is part of the limbic or emotional part of the brain, is where memory is stored. The result is that memory is inevitably stored along with emotions surrounding that memory. In fact, emotions serve as kind of a way of classifying and finding memories. In other words, when you're in a certain mood, it may be very difficult to recall times when you were in a different mood, thus making it very important to keep track of mood changes over time. Otherwise, decisions may get made based on what your mood is at the moment, rather than a more comprehensive sense of how things have been over a period of time.

Goal Setting

Psychiatrists tend to focus on the reduction of symptoms. One prominent psychiatrist, Dr. Gary Sachs, has proposed that, "The ultimate goal of bipolar management should be complete and sustained remission (meaning the absence of significant symptoms), whenever possible..." Dr. Sachs goes on to say, though, that for most people this goal may not be achievable.[1] I would argue that the question of whether this is even a good goal or not needs to be raised, as this book does.

Dr. Sachs points out later in the same article, "Over aggressive management might entail pushing medication doses to intolerable levels...." I suspect a better goal is to medicate in a way that helps reduce mood changes to a point where they are manageable and don't interfere with a successful life.

Treatment

Psychiatrists tend to be interested in using many different approaches to treatment. These treatments may include medications, psychotherapy, behavioral therapy, health interventions, referrals for appropriate non-psychiatric medical assessments, and advising patients on healthy living habits. Even such treatments as Transcranial Magnetic Stimulation (TMS) or Vagal Nerve Stimulation (VNS) could be included. Depending on the nature of the disorder, the severity of symptoms, and level of impairment, a treatment can take place in a number of settings. Options

---

1 http://cat.inist.fr/?aModele=afficheN&cpsidt=14836505

include out-patient treatment, the more intensive partial hospitalization program, or even residential treatment options.

Psychiatrists vary in the extent to which they practice all of these different modalities. Most psychiatrists are comfortable using and monitoring medications, and will usually refer people for psychotherapy. Other types of psychiatric treatment may require consultation with another psychiatrist (such as with TMS).

Psychotherapy

Rochelle I. Frank, PhD

Point Of View

Most clinicians who treat people with bipolar conditions embrace a theoretical model that includes biological, psychological, and social variables. Though often necessary, medication alone usually is not enough. Successful treatments typically target negative symptom reduction and include interventions that will maximize as well as sustain individuals' progress over time. Psychotherapy plays a critical role in educating patients about their condition and the many factors influencing its course. It also teaches skills that can help people overcome disruptions in functioning and improve their overall quality of living.

Integration With Team

The psychotherapist often is the first point of contact for the patient, who initially may have sought help for depression or anxiety. Once a diagnosis of bipolar disorder is made, the psychologist or other therapist (e.g., social worker, marriage and family therapist) plays a crucial role in developing, organizing, and implementing a comprehensive and effective care plan. A collaborative team approach – including psychotherapy, psychiatric care, recreation and exercise, nutrition, and many other aspects of health and wellness – is the key to successful treatment. The patient is the most important member of the team, and collaboration includes family, friends, and other significant individuals who are able to provide support and participate in the plan.

Many therapists in private practice work independently and do not have pre-established relationships with psychiatrists and other key professionals (e.g., personal trainers, professional coaches, nutritionists). Whereas this might not be an issue for most patients, individuals with bipolar conditions benefit greatly from such services, and typically need them to get their lives back in order. Thus, it is important to ask if your therapist has access to these services, and to discuss how to incorporate them into your treatment.

Due to confidentiality laws, it is necessary to provide consent allowing your therapist and others to exchange information about your treatment and progress. Similarly, your therapist might want to meet with individuals to gather important information, including how you were doing prior to episodes of illness. Such contact also requires consent. It is important to talk with your therapist early on about how to best get in touch with her/him; to establish how and when team members will be communicating with each other; the content of such communication; and what, if any, costs will be incurred.

Though patients and professionals ideally come together for periodic "team meetings," this may not be feasible. Fortunately, technology has made collaboration much more possible, though the confidentiality of email and cell phone transmissions cannot be guaranteed. Also, some professionals may not be comfortable utilizing these methods. Regardless of how therapists and other team members choose to communicate, frequent and open exchange of information is central to coordinated and collaborative treatment.

Assessment Process

Standard practice among psychologists begins with a comprehensive assessment of the patient's needs and strengths. Depending on the type of therapy practiced (e.g., cognitive-behavioral, dialectical behavioral, interpersonal social rhythm, psychodynamic), assessment may focus on underlying thoughts and behaviors, coping strategies, former and current relationships, daily schedules, and so forth. Identification of key problem areas (e.g., loss of income, social isolation, insomnia), and specific emotional (e.g., low or expansive mood) and behavioral (e.g., suicidal thoughts) difficulties, leads to clarification of treatment goals and decisions about interventions. Regardless of whether a DSM-IV[1] diagnosis or a narrative description is established, it is important to get a clear and agreed-upon understanding of the issues that will be targeted for treatment.

Assessment often starts during the first telephone conversation, with a brief discussion of the reasons for seeking treatment, impact on current functioning, and identification of resources, supports, and existing services. This conversation provides both therapist and patient with a sense of "goodness of fit" based on personality characteristics, theoretical orientation and professional skills, and offers an op-

---

1 Diagnostic and Statistical Manual of Mental Disorders, Fourth Edition (American Psychiatric Association, 1994

portunity to decide whether or not to schedule an office-based consultation.

Many clinicians, especially those implementing evidence-based treatment (i.e., treatment protocols developed through empirical research, producing consistent positive outcomes), utilize a variety of assessment tools. These range from questionnaires describing personal, family, academic, work, and psychiatric histories, to depression and other symptom inventories. Though important, these instruments do not replace a good face-to-face "clinical interview." The interview includes: discussing information provided on the forms; assessing mental status (e.g., mood, nature and quality of one's thinking and judgment) and current level of functioning (e.g., self-care, school/work performance); and discussing the individual's view of the problems and assessing his/her ability and willingness to participate in treatment. It also is important to identify personal strengths and other resources that bolster treatment outcomes, such as family/social supports, stable income, structured routines, etc. Since many people with bipolar conditions may not have accurate perceptions of their own lives, input from others who know them in various capacities and roles is helpful in providing a context for past and present functioning. Lastly, a discussion of previous treatment efforts and problem solving strategies facilitates informed decisions about current and new interventions.

Goal Setting

Meaningful outcomes derive from specific needs, though the task of developing treatment goals may be confusing and overwhelming. Breaking this task down into short- and long-term targets, developing a "wish list" for change, and thinking about how one's life would be different if problems miraculously disappeared, can be stepping stones toward goal setting.

Common goals might include a reduction in depressive, (hypo)manic, and other symptoms, as well as qualitative improvements in daily functioning. For example, the plan might focus on helping someone resume academics or work, increasing contact with others, and establishing healthy relationships. Health and wellness goals might reflect gaining/losing weight, improving nutrition, and developing an exercise plan. Increasing self-esteem and diminishing the shame that often accompanies mental health problems also are important, though determining one's progress on these dimensions can be difficult. All goals should include identification of clear and measurable outcomes in order to assess progress.

Treatment

In selecting a therapist that is the "best fit" it is important to consider rapport, ability to collaborate, experience, and expertise in treating bipolar conditions. The most positive outcomes seem to be achieved by clinicians who are trained in empirically supported treatments (ESTs).

A longstanding EST is cognitive-behavioral therapy (CBT), which helps people change underlying beliefs and maladaptive behaviors to facilitate reduction of negative depressive and manic symptoms. CBT also is effective with anxiety and obsessive-compulsive symptoms, which often accompany bipolar conditions. Interpersonal social rhythm therapy (IPSRT) facilitates functional and mood stability by examining and restructuring individuals' current activities, sleep-wake cycles, relationships, and situational stressors. Dialectical behavior therapy (DBT) was developed to treat borderline personality disorder, but recent applications also have proven effective in treating bipolar conditions in adults and adolescents. Family-focused treatment was developed for pediatric bipolar disorder, though adult interventions often incorporate family supports to help individuals recognize early warning signs and prevent relapse. Many therapists integrate components of different ESTs to address specific patient needs. Regardless of which therapist or type of treatment you choose, it is important to ask how your progress will be regularly assessed and monitored, since ongoing monitoring has been shown to facilitate the best outcomes.

Relationship Counseling

Maureen Duffy, PhD

Point Of View

Relationships are a central focus area of the Advantage Program and as such putting them "in order" is an important goal. We work with all participants who have direct experience of bipolar to help them face up to any difficulties they might be having in their relationships. We also work with family members and friends to do the same. When relationships are "in order," they can be a source of ongoing support and nurturance for those wanting to live richer, fuller lives. Conversely, relationships that are in "disorder" hold people back from living the lives they want to live.

We help those with direct experience and family members and friends to be accountable for their own actions and reactions in relationships. We help participants imagine the kinds of positive relationships they would like to have with family members and friends and then we help them do the difficult and exciting work of creating those relationships.

Integration With Team

All of the team members share similar values about creating a life worth living. They recognize that achieving *Results Worth Striving For* is both demanding and inspiring. Team members are there to help you with particular challenges and needs that you may have along the way. The relationships therapist and educator coordinate their services with those of the other providers to insure optimal care and success for you and your family members.

Assessment Process

Assessment is a way of helping people figure out where they are at now--what their baseline positions are--so that it will be clearer and easier to get to where they want to be in the future. During the assessment process, you and your family members' hopes for improved relationships will be the foundation. Assessment is only useful when it can help in the process of problem-solving and change.

Relationship assessment is a tool to help you and your family members identify areas of strength as well as areas with room for growth and development. This process is conducted by a licensed mental health professional specifically trained in relationship, marriage, and family issues.

The relationships assessment is a collaborative process between you and your therapist. What this means is that your relationship therapist is not going to assume the stance of expert and tell you what you need to do. You and your family will be fully involved in the process. Your input and that of your family members is critical to successful relationship assessment.

You and your relationship therapist will work together to assess the quality of your relationships and to identify relationship goals along the following dimensions:

◇ Communication

◇ Openness, trust, and honesty
◇ Anger management, conflict management, conflict resolution, and problem-solving
◇ Expressions of affection
◇ Intimacy
◇ Handling emotion and emotional intensity
◇ Emotional self-regulation
◇ Supportiveness and caring within the relationship
◇ Appreciation for self and others in the family
◇ Family-centered approach to living and thriving with bipolar

The initial formal assessment process culminates with the development of a specific relationship improvement plan for you and your family. Your personalized plan will help you to map out the necessary changes that will result in more satisfying, deeper, richer, less conflicted relationships that will be a source of nourishment and support for you all. Throughout the treatment phase, assessment will be a continuous process, drawing from the initial formal assessment and adjusted, as needed.

Goal Setting

The relationship improvement plan is the outcome of the process of relationship life planning. Difficulties in any of the relationship dimensions listed above are suggestive of breaks or ruptures in important relationships. Such disruptions are normal and inevitable in all relationships.

The key is learning how to identify and repair those relationship ruptures as quickly as possible. The relationship therapist will work with you to develop relationship goals that are of particular importance to you and your family.

Everyone's relationships are unique so the relationship plan for you and your family members will be individually tailored. Your relationship therapist will assist you in setting goals that are realistic and manageable. Those goals will include a focus on areas in which you experience the most frequent and intense difficulties and ruptures.

Your therapist will help you identify benchmarks by which you can measure progress towards reaching your relationship goals. Your therapist will also help you and your family members assume shared responsibility for achieving these relationship goals. Through goal setting, you and your family will have an understanding of the steps all of you need to take to have better relationships.

Treatment

Relationships can be improved and relationship ruptures can be repaired. People with direct experience of bipolar are not doomed to have diminished relationships and neither are their family members. Participants will learn evidence-based skills shown to improve the quality of relationships between people with direct experience of bipolar and their family members.

General skills that participants will learn include the following:

  ◇ Increasing the frequency of positive interactions with each other.

○ Decreasing criticism, fault-finding, blaming, and expressions of exasperation.

○ Learning how to handle anxiety better through practices of personal self-regulation--staying calm and re-
acting to situations as thoughtfully and tranquilly as
possible.

○ Increasing problem-solving behaviors and decreasing
panic and intense emotional reactions.

○ Setting realistic expectations for one another.

Individualized relationship education and therapy is
designed to meet the unique needs of each person with direct experience of bipolar and their circle of family and
friends.

Mind Skills Coaching

Brian Weller

Point Of View

"The greatest discovery of my generation is that man can alter his life simply by altering his attitude of mind."

- James Truslow Adams[1]

Mind Skills training is an adventure! It offers fresh and time honored techniques to unlock our power to be fully alive. The mind is extremely powerful. It is so powerful and intimate to us that we forget that it requires great skill to use it effectively. This is especially true for those with a bipolar condition.

Some of the greatest minds in history have displayed bipolar traits. When we reflect on the lives and contributions of people like Ludwig van Beethoven, Buzz Aldrin, Ernest Hemingway, Winston Churchill, and Florence Nightingale, what singles them out for greatness is that they lived their "bipolar condition" as an advantage. This creative attitude or point of view is what made the difference in their own lives, but more importantly, made a difference to us all. We can learn from them. The secret is to know your purpose and get organized to achieve it by managing your mind.

Exercising the mind and developing skills is as impor-tant as developing the body, if not more so. Our mental abili-

---

1 American writer and historian - 1878-1949

ties are central to our ability to get *Bipolar In Order*. Without a well developed mind, we do not have the strength to control our minds when put under duress. Just as a weak body breaks down when it needs to do heavy lifting, an undeveloped mind breaks down when under stress. Depression, mania, hallucinations, and delusions are the greatest mental stressors known to man. It takes a well developed mind to overcome them.

Integration With Team

The Mind Skills Coach reinforces the learning techniques and mental strategies which support the work of the entire program. Mind Mapping that the client created in brainstorming sessions or in visioning their Life Plan can be shown and shared with others, bringing them closer to the inner world of the client.

A mind skills coach creates specific exercises to fulfill the goals outlined by other team members. For example, in the same way that the fitness coach can suggest exercises based on a more intimate knowledge of the client's skill set, the mind skills coach can find the best exercises to accomplish the goals set out by the psychotherapist for relaxation, meditation, or other goals.

The mind skills coach can also give input to the other team members about changes in the client's ability to perform the exercises. These changes can be indicative of struggles that other team members are not aware of and can help them to make adjustments in their approach.

Assessment Process

An accurate assessment of the client's mental skill level and ability is attained through the use of questionnaires and inventories to test and assess attitude, memory, creativity, brainstorming, ability to change state from rapid thinking to calm, and the client's willingness to embark on personal change.

An abundance of exercises exist to assess current abilities as well as progress along the path to greater skills. Like physical tests for strength, the mental tests are very specific in measurement and there are clear skill levels that can be compared to norms for both the bipolar population and so called "normal" people.

Goal Setting

Goals can be both standalone and necessary components of goals in other areas of the life plan. Spiritual goals can be greatly facilitated by developing meditation skills, for example.

When looking at the physical, mental, emotional, spiritual, relationships, and career/financial goals, it is important to keep in mind what mind skills need to be practiced in order to achieve them. While it is nice to be able to increase memory or think faster, it is critical to develop such skills if you have career goals that require them.

Treatment

Turning good intentions into real and lasting change builds the confidence essential for putting *Bipolar In Order*. Coaching is essentially a facilitation process for people to integrate and establish skills. These skills include Mind Mapping, memory strategies for short and long term recall, mindset and attitude coaching, creativity processes, personal change work, and mental rehearsal techniques.

Coaching is done both one-to-one and in groups. It can be done in person, over the phone, or via the internet. It is usually done in forty five minute to one hour sessions and can be as frequent as weekly, but should be at least once a month if the skills are going to be reinforced enough to hold.

Daily practice, and some times multiple times a day, are necessary for the mind to create the habits needed for success. Mental exercises seem very simple on the surface, but we know the mind's tendency to avoid change easily rivals the body's. It takes discipline to keep up the practice.

Adherence can be greatly helped by working with friends and family or in support group settings. It can also make a huge difference to have one-to-one sessions with a coach.

Mind Skills coaching includes:

- Check-in to reaffirm purpose, goals and actions - "What am I creating in my daily life and why?"
- Exploration - "How am I doing?" Clients explore their issues, questions, and concerns that have arisen dur-

ing the week. The coach clarifies them so that clients can reset their goals. In group sessions, these issues are explored with the group and invariably others share similar or related issues.

⬡ Tune up - Tuning up the Mind Skills routines so that they fit more successfully into a clients' work, leisure, and home life.

⬡ Development - The coach gives hands-on training to build skills to new levels of competence and effectiveness.

⬡ Support - Individual and group support to help clients to stay on the path.

Spiritual Counseling

Scott Sullender, PhD

Point Of View

Depression and bipolar are multi dimensional conditions. It affects one's emotions, one's thoughts, one's physical health, one's relationships, one's will power and, of course, one's spiritual life. You might say that depression is a whole person disorder or condition.

We call depression an affective disorder, which means that it is primarily a condition that damages one's mood or emotions. Yet, those who struggle with depression know full well that it is much more than that and depression must be and is best addressed on multiple levels.

Depression, or its cousin mania, affects our spirituality. Depression becomes like a filter on our glasses that prevents or colors how we experience our spiritual life. In times of depression or since becoming depressed, we may come to feel that God is now far away or silent or angry. It may be harder to pray or meditate when the depression is intense. It may be difficult to feel at peace, to forgive others, to see any hope in the future, to feel any sense of genuine gratitude, or to find a sense of purpose in life. Depression or bipolar condition can damage or alter our spiritual life, even as it influences every other part of life.

Yet, it is also true that periods of depression may also be times when we have a rich opportunity to strengthen our spiritual life in new ways. The very depression that seemingly prevents us from seeing God may actually force us to see God in a new way, and to discover a deeper, more profound spirituality. This is the message of many of the mystics and saints from both western and eastern religious traditions. Sometimes it is precisely through these periods of what St. John of the Cross, called the "Dark Night of the Soul" that God can be experienced in renewed and powerful ways.

Spiritual practices are not a substitute for psychotherapy, medication or other related services if needed. Spiritual counseling can, however, be a supplemental resource that will help strengthen the spiritual arm of our battle with depression. It can be one component, sometimes even a very significant component in a total person approach to depression.

Integration With Team

Some of the aspects of a spiritual treatment for depression do overlap with other components of the total Advantage Program. For example, one's cognitions or thinking patterns can be addressed both by a cognitive therapist and by a spiritual counselor. This is so because many of the meta-cognitions or assumptions we make about life, ourselves, or our future are basically theological or philosophical in nature. Similarly, forgiveness can be addressed both in relationship therapy and in conversations with a spiritual counselor, depending on the context of one's forgiveness work.

Thus, spiritual counselors need to be in regular contact and consultation with the other professionals working as a team.

Assessment Process

The assessment process begins by helping the client review his or her spiritual journey--its ups and downs, the moments of power, surrender and transformation, and times of death and rebirth. The assessment will include both the content of one's spirituality and the degree of active practice of one's faith tradition. Your spirituality is your spirituality! The role of the spiritual counselor is not to impose or challenge the client's faith tradition. The counselor's role is to help the counselee examine and/or renew his or her own spiritual walk. Depression or any kind of so called mental illness often does create a "crisis of faith," calling forth from us a re-examination and then a revitalization of our faith tradition.

In addition to conversation, there are several written assessment tools that can be helpful, including "Forgiveness Survey" and the "Spiritual Assessment Scale." Some of the topics or themes assessed in these scales include: meaningfulness of life, purpose of suffering, mindfulness attitude, self-forgiveness and forgiveness of others, gratitude and thanksgiving, presence of the Divine, connection to a spiritual community, strength of hope, inner peace or serenity, personal worth or significance, perfectionism and grace, and a sense of calling or purpose in life. Along the way, a spiritual counselor or spiritual director will teach the counselee a variety of spiritual practices designed, if employed regularly, to strengthen the individual's battle against depression.

Goal Setting

The goal is simple enough: to revitalize your spiritual life and use that revitalization to strengthen your battle with depression and mania. In particular spiritual counseling aims to increase the following:

○ A sense of purpose or meaningfulness of life
○ An ability to forgive self and others
○ An ability to feel and sustain gratitude
○ A sense of connectedness to a spiritual community
○ A sense of personal worth and significance
○ An awareness of the presence of God
○ A sense of hope regarding the future
○ A sense of inner peace or serenity in the face of addictions
○ The use of prayer, meditation and other spiritual practices

Treatment

Our treatment regimen normally includes a series of conversations with a qualified spiritual counselor. Our definition of "qualified" is a professional with both academic and clinical training in both psychology/counseling and theology/spirituality. It also includes a person who does not work in isolation, but is accountable to and consultative with a team of interdisciplinary professionals. We respect the training and program of the American Association of Pastoral Counselors.[1] We also respect spiritual directors who are members of Spiritual Directors International.[2]

During our treatment, the spiritual counselor will discuss the various components of spirituality, noted above in the assessment phase. The counselor will then explore the blocks that prevent the client from realizing a fuller spirituality. We will help the client tap into the various, perhaps hidden spiritual resources within his or her life that can be useful in this enterprise. Spiritual counselors normally assign homework, usually in the form of various spiritual practices and actively coach clients through the successful use of these practices.

Spiritual counselors will also help clients self-assess on a regular basis to make sure the client is achieving the results he or she desires.

---

1 http://www.aapc.org

2 http://www.sdiworld.org

Family & Friends

James W. Jordan, Jr.

Point Of View

Family support is vital to achieving *Results Worth Striving For*. As family members, we are advocates, but also emotionally invested loved-ones who want wellness and happiness for our family as a whole. We also want to see the success of each member of our family. A well-informed family member who is engaged in the process can be a key component of success.

Family members develop a profound understanding that each individual must express self-determination as the foundation of personal growth and true change. One family member's diagnosis does not make the rest of the family perfect. Family members will have to set their own goals of growth and understanding too. Ultimately, there is only one person we can change, and that is ourselves.

Integration With Team

Family members offer critical and sometimes otherwise missing information to the team. The family member offers first-hand experience in the long-term support of a client working toward wellness, having personally witnessed personality and mood changes along with diagnosis-related behaviors and symptoms. Where the client may not fully agree with assessments or treatments advocated by the other team members, the family member can provide another point of view in accepting or rejecting ideas for treatment.

The family embarks on an educational adventure by taking part in this journey. By seeking out information, taking workshops, attending therapy sessions, and participating with the team members, the family is included and essential to success. Learning as much as we can about our own thoughts and actions and the effect these have on family dynamics will lead family members on their own journey of personal growth.

Assessment Process

Assessments provided by a family member are invaluable to the team and the client's eventual wellness. A family member can speak to the unique challenges and responsibilities inherent to the current family situation. The family member contributes insights and information to the team that do not turn up in the other assessments.

Where there is a disparity between what the client reports and what the family observes on a daily basis, the assessment process will help to clarify the situation. Many family members remark that they wish the treating psychiatrist or therapist could come home with them. When clients leave out information, present well, and are delusional regarding their own state of well being, the therapist is being asked by the client to treat a mythological person. The family lives with the truth on a daily basis.

The client and family can only work together on the Life Plan when there is agreement about where they are on the map. The assessment phase serves that purpose for the entire family.

Goal Setting

The unique perspective of a family member enables the client or the team to evaluate if goals are mindful of the client's living arrangements, relationships, and family responsibilities.

The family works to recognize what it will take to maintain appropriate balance and dynamics while undergoing personal growth and change. Goal setting clarifies the role of individual family members in relationship to the client's own goals.

Family relationship dynamics will become very evident when setting goals. This is why education and counseling in relationships is important to the success of any Life Plan. The family accepts that the client's goals include transition stages of change and growth as part of an organized plan. When setting goals it is important to admit that each individual within the family group does not have the same view of progress or of the future. These differences will have to be reconciled or at least acknowledged for optimum outcomes to be achieved by the entire family.

Treatment

While the family may not consider themselves to be in treatment with the client, the contributions that they can make to the success of the treatment phase are considerable. Families that thrive do so in part because of their ability to move away from the concept of illness. An important part of the treatment process is accepting that well-being, health, and confidence will to return to the family unit.

The client is asked to acknowledge that family members are learning new information and undergoing a process of change almost equal to their own. For this reason, a spirit of cooperation, understanding, and acceptance of each others struggles and pitfalls is essential. Acceptance, openness, and improved communication skills will help to reduce the tendency to take on unhelpful roles, like surveillance or deception.

Everything that is accomplished in therapy should not be undone when the client arrives back in the family unit. The family can avoid becoming an unwitting source of confusion by participating with the integrated team from the very beginning. The family is essential to the original assessments and the on-going process.

Developing patience cannot be understated. Personal growth doesn't happen overnight. It takes time to assimilate new information and tools, incorporate them into our thinking, and put them into practice. During on-going treatment it is important for the family to support the goals and to not expect the client to change lifetime habits immediately.

Addictions Counseling

Michael R. Edelstein, PhD

Point Of View

REBT[1] offers an alternative to the conventional view of addictions. No one is powerless over their drug/alcohol abuse, no matter what their past or current circumstances happen to be.

Rather, the immediate cause of addictions lies with the thoughts, beliefs, ideas in your head--what you tell yourself--immediately before you drink, overeat, smoke, or shoot up. Unrealistic thinking is the essential cause of addiction, and such thinking takes the form of "must's," "awful's," and "can't-stand-it's." By changing the thinking process, addictive behavior can be overcome. "I MUST get high! It's AWFUL to be deprived! I CAN'T STAND discomfort!" is the refrain of those addicted. Such "musty" notions lead to escape into drugs.

Individuals addict themselves to pleasurable experiences to escape discomfort, enhance good feelings, or both. Improving performance, fitting in with peers, and differentiating oneself from other groups (especially parents) are specific instances of these larger goals.

When you feel depressed, for example, you may drink excessively to drown these feelings. The next morning

---

1 Rational Emotive Bahavior Therapy - http://www.rebtnetwork.org/

you may get depressed about your previous night's self-destructive behavior. This pattern illustrates how individuals with emotional and addiction problems often use addictions to escape their emotional difficulties. Emotional problems may also be created in response to addictions. This vicious circle has been labeled "dual diagnosis."

The addiction may be addressed separately from the emotional problem or in conjunction with it, depending on the circumstances of the client, the problem, or the therapeutic interaction.

Using addictions to escape disturbed emotions has also been labeled "self-medication." In other words, the individual drank in response to the initial depression as a way to "medicate" it away or escape from it. Prescription drugs may be used for this purpose, as well.

Integration With Team

"Epidemiological data from several countries show that substance abuse or dependence is common (25–50%) among persons disabled by severe mental disorders such as schizophrenia, bipolar disorder or chronic depression."[1] Thus the importance of including addiction counseling as a part of the process.

The addiction counselor shares valuable insight with the other team members. For example, a report from the addiction counselor regarding resumed drug usage will help the psychotherapist understand any noted behavioral

1 Psychiatry, Volume 3, Issue 10, Pages 60-63 R.DRAKE

changes in the client. The reverse can also be true in that the addiction counselor can point out any behaviors typical of withdrawal.

Shared insight is reciprocal. Reports from other team members can facilitate the counselor's understanding of the particular triggers that led to addictive behaviors. Without communication between team members, the client loses important guidance.

Assessment Process

The first step in the assessment process involves understanding the client's perspective on the problem. This includes appreciating the circumstances and context of the problem and evaluating the client's long- and short-term goals. Some clients are clear that they drink or get high excessively, for example, and wish to quit for good. Others are unclear about whether they're overdoing it. Those who are convinced they're addicted, may ask whether abstinence or moderation makes sense for them. Some clients may have a mix of addiction and emotional disturbance and may not know how these are related. Others may have their addiction as a factor in the larger context of relationship difficulties.

The next step involves assessing which problem to address first. Although some clients show impatience and wish to address all their problems immediately, this is not possible. Do we address their addiction problem, emotional problem, or relationship problem initially? It's probably best to have the client decide. Simply and directly state the question: "which problem would you like to start with?" If the client is indifferent, then the therapist can determine which seems most pressing, and start with that. For example, if the client's partner has delivered an ultimatum, e.g., "If you get high again, I'm leaving," then under most circumstances it's prudent to focus immediately on helping the client to abstain.

The next step involves the education process: explaining how addiction is defined, where addictions come from, and how the fundamentals of the change process operate. REBT involves the backbone of our treatment. This approach is explained along with recommending further reading including *Three Minute Therapy*[1] by this author and *When AA Doesn't Work for You*[2] by Albert Ellis and Emmett Velten.

Goal Setting

Clients tend to have a variety of long-, medium-, and short-term goals in the process of overcoming an addiction. The most common long-term goal involves either quitting for good or moderation. Variations on this involve a middle-term goal of abstaining for a predetermined period followed by long-term moderation. Others begin with the long-term goal of moderation, and should this fail, abstinence as the default.

When a client is unsure about whether moderating or abstaining from drinking is reasonable, a look at history often provides the answer. Many compulsive drinkers have a

---

1 Edelstein, Dr. Michael R., Three Minute Therapy, 1997, Glenbridge Publishing, Colorado
www.threeminutetherapy.com

2 Ellis, Albert, and Velten, E., When AA Doesn't Work for You, 1992, Barricade Books, NY

history of attempting moderation and failing multiple times. This points to abstinence as probably the best solution.

"Do I reach my final goal by abstaining or tapering?," involves a common issue, especially for smokers. Since there is no perfect way of determining the answer in advance, I recommend taking a best guess at which is likely to be successful, then experimenting with it.

A final factor involved with overcoming addictions involves time frames for each step in the process. This is an individual choice based on history, including past failures and successes, and the consequences the addicted individual faces by continuing the self-defeating behavior. Some individuals quit overnight. Others take months or years of patience, persistence, learning from mistakes, relapses, and refusing to give up, before they ultimately succeed.

Treatment

REBT addiction counseling generally is conducted in-person or by phone. The average course of treatment involves 8-10 sessions, beginning with sessions weekly. As the client masters the REBT concepts and tools, and gets in control of the addictive behavior, sessions tend to get spread out over a few weeks, then monthly.

REBT follows an educational teacher-student, rather than a medical doctor-patient, model with sessions resembling a tutorial. After the initial assessment process described above, the therapist teaches the client concepts and strategies immediately applicable to the client's problem. Each session concludes with specific collaboratively-devised exercises for the client to practice daily between sessions. The following session begins by reviewing the homework, with modifications added based on the client's successes and failures with it during the week. If the client has immediate questions or concerns, addressing these would take precedence over the usual structure, with the homework reviewed after this.

The bulk of each session consists of reviewing tools and strategies the client may use in overcoming the addiction. These include: vividly reading a disadvantages list, refuting rationalizations, Three Minute Exercises, setting goals with rewards and penalties, and bibliotherapy. The client is encouraged to experiment with a variety of these to discover which ones prove most effective.

Career Management Counseling

Maria Chang-Calderon, PhD(c), MSHR

Point Of View

Employment, well-being, and quality of life are closely tied for several reasons. Gainful employment contributes to financial freedom, the ability to pay for wants and needs, and the enjoyment of physical, mental, emotional, and spiritual well-being. Predictors of success at work include employment history, psychiatric diagnosis, and the ability to manage one's condition. An Advantage Program career management counselor is not looking to spell out limitations; they are there to help create the life you want.

Career management counseling does not include job placement services; however, it addresses how to stay competitively employed. This entails assessing one's strengths, weaknesses, and workplace conditions. Career coaching is based on identifying immediate problems and successes in the workplace and finding the indicators that will help an individual maintain or improve his/her performance.

If there are issues due to stigma that need to be dealt with in the workplace, the career management counselor can help clients identify what resources are available to them to ensure their rights are protected. The counselor encourages clients to make use of the Integrated Team, managing their condition with the help of trusted therapists, friends, family, and health care providers.

Integration With Team

Success at work requires having positive work relationships and a network of support outside the workplace. The clients will be guided to identify persons that can support them if they feel that fluctuations in energy levels, depression, or symptoms of mania require acknowledgement and consideration. It is helpful to keep the therapist and other team members informed about personal challenges, adverse reactions to various conditions, or negative symptoms like issues related to secondary effects of medications. In the same way, team members will need to be advised if positive changes occur that may contribute to a better work experience.

This information can help to fine tune suggestions by therapists and create a more realistic discussion by the entire team regarding work place issues and plans for changing career paths. Improved strength in other areas will provide a sound foundation for change in the workplace if the client chooses to undertake that challenge.

Assessment Process

The assessment process requires the client to create an inventory list of strengths and weaknesses with the help of a career management professional. This paves the way to build on strengths as a foundation for enhanced performance.

There are several assessment tools that identify strengths and increase self-awareness. Three recommended assessment tools include the Myers Briggs Type Indicator (MBTI) personality test, 360 Degree Review, and the Big Five Personality Test. The Myers Briggs Type Indicator (MBTI) allows clients to learn more about themselves and career options. The 360 Degree Review allows the client to obtain input from fellow employees from all hierarchical levels. The Big Five Personality Test is another assessment that is not strictly career-oriented, but provides insight that can be applied to careers, such as how one ranks in the following scales: close-minded vs. open to new experiences, disorganized vs. conscientious, introverted vs. extraverted, disagreeable vs. agreeable, and calm vs. high strung. A career management counselor will help to identify which assessment tool would be best for each individual from the many that are available and discuss the meaning of the results.

Goal Setting

Career goals must be aligned with one's values, preferences, knowledge, skills, and abilities in order to develop a career maintenance and/or development plan that will result in goals being met. Once an individual's inventory of strengths and weaknesses has been discussed, it is necessary to discuss short- and long-term goals and how they can be met by taking steps to build on what is already working. The goal setting process should include a discussion with trusted advisors, friends and/or relatives to ensure the goals are SMART (Specific, Measurable, Achievable, Realistic and Time-framed). Discussing your goals with trusted individuals within your support network can lead to obtaining valuable feedback that will help further refine your career goals to ensure success.

Treatment

Career management counseling services are individualized sessions requiring meeting with the advisor at least once a week in the beginning and less frequent once the plan has been fully implemented. Sessions are conducted by phone or in person. E-mail sessions are discouraged because having a flow of dialogue is important to understand the context of the problem and to consult appropriately. In addition, participating in an employment support group that addresses common employment issues can be beneficial.

Financial Coaching

Denise K. Hughes, M.A.

Point Of View

Money touches every aspect of our lives. Our bank account influences our choice of the car we drive, the size of our house, the neighborhood we live in, schools our children attend, grocery stores we frequent, the healthcare insurance we choose, and much more.

Control, competence, and confidence in our money management creates well being. Benefits of practicing financially mature behaviors include peace of mind, a sense of security, freedom for greater choices, increased life energy, and a good night's rest, free of worry.

The reverse is certainly true, as well. When our financial affairs are not "in order," we are left feeling inadequate, confused, and out of control. The result is even greater stress, which includes the pressure to earn more, conflicts within our relationships, and a deep sense of lack. Eventually, this chronic level of financial strain brings us to our knees and places us in survival mode on Maslow's hierarchy of needs. Over time, this type of continuous assault will break us down physically, mentally, emotionally, and spiritually.

Many of us come from family and educational systems that have not prepared us for even the most basic func-

tions of money management. Money remains one of our society's most taboo topics of conversation. We talk more easily
about sex.

Couple depression or mania with a lack of understanding of money handling and even more problems will
arise. Using money as a device to feel better, elevate one's
mood, or express an expansive mood are all ways that can
drain one's bank account and assets.

To support you in discovering your personal recipe
for financial success, I want to share with you, *secrets of financially successful people:*[1]

Financially successful people control their day to day
finances in order to afford things that bring them satisfaction
and enjoyment. In practical terms, this means creating a cash
flow plan to help set priorities and stay within boundaries in
order to get more of what they want in life. More freedom,
more fun, and more joy are all outcomes of mindful spend-
ing.

Financially successful people are in the "know" when
it comes to their finances. They know their credit score, the
interest rates on their mortgages, debt balances, and how to
protect themselves from fraud and scams. They initiate taking steps toward financial literacy.

Financially successful people create the habit of sav-
ing and investing money. They realize that small steps each
month add up to big dollars down the road. They understand the concept of dollar cost averaging and laddering.

1 http://www.50fabulous.com/columns/view/secrets_of_financially_successful_people/

Financially successful people protect their assets in order to prevent financial disasters caused by catastrophic illness or personal tragedies. They insure themselves with adequate coverage and take balanced risks.

Financially successful people embrace certain mind-sets. They live in the space of possibility and gratitude. They are able to delay gratification and hold both short- and long-term visions for what they want in life. Their dollars nourish their highest values.

Integration With Team

A financial coach and consultant is an important part of the team process in supporting financial wellness. This may mean strategizing with team members on how to balance resources with lifestyle choices in order to maximize *Results Worth Striving For*.

A team approach is valuable in order to offer holistic support to work through limiting beliefs and emotional blocks that get in the way of financial goals. Misleading financial concepts that present in one life area, will present in other areas as well. An integrated approach best supports a breakthrough in misconceptions regarding money as well as strengthening healthy behavioral habits.

Assessment Process

Part I of the assessment process pertains to money mastery skills that help clients reach their full potential. These skills include cash flow management; strategies to fully fund emergency, savings, and investment accounts; as well as strategies to eliminate any unsecured debt. This step also includes an appraisal of mechanisms of asset protection one may need to have in place, such as various insurances and a living trust.

Part II of the assessment will focus on the attitudes and behaviors one brings to their relationship with money. Behaviors consist of one's thoughts, feelings, and actions which are motivated by underlying beliefs. The assessment process will identify both healthy and un-healthy behaviors one has with money and the consequences of each behavior.

Goal Setting

Financially successful people create a written plan to help them get from point A to point B. Examples of this may be a plan to buy a home, to fund our children's education, or to retire comfortably. A written plan gives a sense of direction and points to milestones along the journey. It also serves as a compass to re-navigate when we get off course.

Goal setting is highly individualized. Financial goals are defined by the client and supported by the assessment process. Each goal will be based on the acronym SMART: Specific, Measurable, Achievable, Realistic, And Timely. The Financial Coach and client will co-create a step by step plan to help the client achieve desired results.

Examples of financial goals might be:

◌ Eliminate $6000 of debt over the next 12 months, by paying $500 more a month towards these debts. Find a way to get this extra money by taking on part-time work or a creative project to support this goal.

○ Find a good referral to a financial planner to help support me in knowing what it takes to meet both my short- and long-term goals. Complete this in one month.

○ Create a cash flow plan, track against that plan, and analyze how well the goals are achieved. Take the insights learned into the following month with the intention of doing better.

Treatment

Treatment plans are client specific and based on the agreed upon goals for the course of session work. Generally speaking, a treatment plan may consist of the following processes and concepts:

○ Move out of the money fog - Gaining clarity is the first step in the process. Insight allows one to operate from a perspective based on reality. In regards to money, one needs to be cognizant about the entire financial picture. This includes cash flow, savings, investments, debts, all property loans, income, etc.

○ Take action - The goal is to bring the behaviors of respect, mindfulness, and stewardship to one's finances.

○ Create healthy money habits - The desired outcome is to be in a place of control, ease, and peace when it comes to money.

Generally speaking, money coaching sessions consist of bi-monthly appointments. Session appointments are focused on both process and outcome. Homework assignments, requiring about one hour per week are also required.

Physical Rehabilitation Therapy

Justin Liu, MD

Point Of View

In today's world of immediate gratification, individuals with physical or emotional ailments often seek medical attention with the expectation that a doctor will be able to provide them with a magical pill or medical procedure that will miraculously alleviate all their symptoms instantly. To approach medical treatment with this mentality is usually not realistic or fruitful. As advanced as modern medicine has become, successful treatment of more complicated functionally-impairing conditions requires careful planning and effort by both the physician and the patient.

Regardless of whether an individual has sustained a loss of function due to deconditioning from inactivity or a physical injury from an accident, any loss of function that disrupts a person's ability to participate in the usual daily activities is highly traumatic to the body and mind. Because of this, it is vital to acknowledge the global effect mental illness and physical injury can have on a person's overall well-being. Prolonged physical debility can lead directly to negatively affecting a person's self-image and mood. Conversely, poor mental health can severely impact a person's ability to properly heal and regain lost function.

With the close tie between a person's physical and mental health, it quickly becomes evident that physicians must not make the mistake of treating the mind and body as two separate entities. A successful approach to an individual's global well-being requires that a plan of care be developed with the deeper understanding that the treatment plan's objective is to ultimately promote physical and mental health simultaneously.

Integration With Team

A medical doctor specializing in Physical Medicine & Rehabilitation (PM&R) will play an important role in the recovery process for an individual who has lost the ability to perform his or her activities of daily living. The PM&R physician will help individuals develop a custom-tailored activity program. Often times, the PM&R Physician will design a comprehensive program that ties in specialists from various other fields. Physical Therapists, Occupational Therapists, Recreational Therapists, Nutritionists, and Fitness coaches are often some of the key disciplines that a PM&R Physician will incorporate into the personalized treatment plan for a specific individual. The PM&R Physician will ultimately help guide and direct what activities these specific specialties should focus on with a patient. Specific body biomechanical guidelines are prescribed by the PM&R Physician to help prevent physical injury to the patient.

Assessment Process

Before a physical activity program is started, a PM&R Physician should perform a thorough pre-exercise assessment. As part of this process, a comprehensive History &

Physical examination should be done. Key elements that should be detailed during this exam will include an in-depth look at the individual's prior medical history and uncovering the acute physical issues as well as the subacute chronic issues that are impacting the patient. Family medical history and assessment of the patient's substance use history (i.e. nicotine, alcohol, prescription/non-prescription drugs) are also important variables to consider. A thorough physical examination with focus on musculoskeletal and neurological testing must be completed. A baseline set of blood tests and an electrocardiogram may also be obtained to ensure that the patient does not have other underlying medical conditions that could limit activity. Such conditions like anemia, electrolyte disturbances, dehydration, or arrhythmias must be adequately addressed before an individual can safely embark on a program of regimented physical activity.

Another essential part of the assessment process will be the functional evaluation. The PM&R Physician should accurately determine what the patient's current functional status is. The individual's physical endurance and ability to perform basic activities of daily living should be looked at in detail. In tailoring a program for a patient, it is imperative to see how much function a patient has lost over a recent interim of time. This information will be useful in deciding how to set appropriate and useful goals for the patient.

Goal Setting

Once an accurate assessment of an individual's current physical condition has been done, the PM&R Physician can help design an activity program specific to the patient's strengths and weaknesses. The idea is to design a therapeutic exercise regimen that is neither too easy nor too difficult for the patient. The program must also provide an appropriate challenge to the patient from both a physical and cognitive standpoint. Another vital factor is to create a routine that is dynamic and entertaining for the individual. No one likes performing activities that are repetitive or dull. Various therapy modalities should therefore be used to help keep things from becoming monotonous. Unless it is medically contraindicated, I feel it is beneficial to have patients participate in a variety of activities: from isometric weight-training activities to isodynamic aerobic-type activities to more alternative use of interactive gaming technologies like the Nintendo Wii. The key is to be creative while never losing sight of the primary objective of assisting the patient to regain a sense of physical and mental well-being through a structured program of progressively increasing physical activity.

When designing the exercise regimen, it is important to check in at regular intervals with the patient and his or her Rehab Therapist or Fitness Coach to see how a patient is doing in reaching a specific goal. It is crucial that the goals set for an individual are realistic and actually attainable. Functional goals should not be rigid. Depending on progress, new goals can always be set. It is paramount to always remember that goals, like the individuals themselves, need to always evolve and not remain static.

Treatment

As the individual continues on his regimen of therapeutic exercises, the PM&R Physician will need to constantly maintain lines of communication with the patient. Feedback on how the patient feels physically and emotionally should be assessed at regular intervals. To ensure that the patient does not develop a physical barrier to hinder his or her progress with the program, it is critical that the PM&R Physician assess the patient's overall pain levels and provide appropriate treatment in an efficient manner. In an effective therapy program, there are often noticeable physiologic and emotional changes that occur. Blood pressure and blood sugars often improve with weight loss and improved overall fitness. Patients who struggle with insomnia start to have improved sleep-wake cycles with a structured exercise routine. Individuals who are on psychotropic medications for depression and mania begin to notice improvement of their overall mood, self-image, and energy levels. As the PM&R Physician who is checking in and monitoring all of these positive changes, appropriate medical management must concurrently be provided. Necessary coordination and discussion with the patient's Primary Care Physician, Psychiatrist, and other treating specialist physicians must be done to ensure that the patient's various medications are appropriately lowered or tapered off based on the noted physical and emotional changes.

Nutrition Counseling

Ruth Leyse-Wallace, PhD, RD

Point Of View

The mind and brain, as well as the body, need adequate nutritional intake for wellness and optimum functioning. Even though nutrition is only one factor in mental and physical health, it is highly influential for both mind and body. It is also quite easily improved and should be included in any effort to sustain mental health. A complete and sufficient array of nutrients are needed for:

- an energy supply
- transporting and transforming food into the energy form usable by the physical body and brain
- creating enzymes, hormones, bone, muscle, neurotransmitters, and immune system
- facilitating the expression of DNA
- coping with stress

Memory, cognition, attention span, aggression, irritability, feelings of well being, and mental energy may be affected by nutritional status. Consuming too few of the necessary nutrients affects so many bodily systems it is not surprising that poor nutrition decreases the quality of life in both obvious and subtle ways. Nutrients include:

- carbohydrates
- essential fatty acids
- amino acids

◇ folic acid and other B vitamins
◇ vitamin C
◇ minerals such as chromium, zinc, and iron

Bipolar disorder and depression may influence whether an individual consumes an adequate supply of foods and the nutrients they supply. The manic state can lead to distraction in which less attention is given to the preparation of adequate foods. Increased activity during this phase requires additional nutritional needs that are not always met. Depression can lead to a lack of energy and motivation for eating adequately, leading to weight gain or loss and associated health issues.

Medications may interact with nutrient intake or metabolism and affect the body's use of nutrients. Toxicity may result from excess intake of some nutrients, which in turn can affect mental function.

Often, the scientific evidence linking nutrition to mental health is correlational in nature. Cause and effect links are scientifically difficult in both nutrition and mental health research. However, scientists around the world publish new research results monthly that contribute to knowledge in these areas.

Integration With Team

One function of the nutritionist is to determine a client's nutritional status and bring to the attention of the team any potential problems or special needs. Some nutrition issues may need the coordination of the nutritionist, the physician, activity therapist, pharmacist, and other professionals on the team. Family members also support ongoing solutions.

The nutritionist assists a client with setting nutrition goals and creating a plan to attain them. Follow-up meetings generally lead to greater progress than trying to go it alone.

The nutritionist also acts as a resource for the team, the client, and the family. Providing current, scientifically-based, practical information about nutrition can provide the rationale for nutritional goals and plans. For example, in the past a prescription for a monoamine oxidase inhibitor [MAOI] required a low tyramine diet to prevent a hypertensive crisis. Now administration by patch instead of orally, at some doses, does not require following the diet.

Assessment Process

Findings during the initial interview are evaluated by the nutritionist, discussed with the client, and shared with the team members. Assessment of initial nutritional status includes an interview by the nutritionist to gather information concerning:

- usual food, beverage, and supplement intake
- current weight and recent weight changes
- physical problems with eating (dental health for example)
- the need for a nutrition-focused physical examination (and performance of the exam if needed)
- biochemical laboratory testing to validate observations and findings
- presence of diarrhea or constipation

◌ possible interactions between medications and nutritional status or individual nutrients

◌ medical issues that may affect or be affected by nutrition

◌ presence of nutritional risk factors related to family history (bipolar disorder, diabetes, etc)

◌ subjective symptoms felt by the client to be affecting intake or nutritional status (frequent nausea or extreme fatigue, among others)

Results of laboratory tests will be evaluated and discussed when they are complete. They will then be integrated into goal-setting and determining a treatment plan. The client's priorities and preferences will be an integral part of goals and treatment planning.

Reassessment and follow-up will occur at appropriate intervals for discovering if nutritional status has changed in the desired direction. For example, it may take one to several weeks for a supplement to promote a change in an enzyme level.

Goal Setting

Goals are statements of behavior; actions to be undertaken with commitment for obtaining a nutritional intake that will support the desired mental and physical health. Individualized goals in relation to nutrition will be based on the nutritional assessment as well as each client's personal interests and life situation.

Goals may be short- or long-term. Goals that are stated simply with a single focus are preferable to complex goals. The best goals are those that can be clearly evaluated. "Eating better" isn't as easily evaluated as "eat three times per day instead of one meal per day."

An individual may have a few or several goals. Certain goals may be addressed one at a time and achieved relatively quickly. Other goals entail changing lifelong habits and will require longer periods of time because readiness to change is influenced by many factors. Goals that involve lifestyle may require several interim goals. Simplistically put, if the desired life style goal is to lose 25 pounds, the first interim goal could be to limit sugar intake. To that end, a second interim goal could be to stop buying a candy bar from the vending machine everyday at break.

Treatment

A treatment regimen will reflect an individual's goals and plans for how best achieve them. It will be developed by the treatment team and the client. The nutrition treatment regimen may include a food plan, supplements, self-monitoring, and education. Treatment may also include assistance from family and friends. Decisions regarding activities that involve food may have to be addressed. Consideration regarding activities that don't involve food may also need to be taken into account.

Monitoring an individual's progress in reaching his/ her goals and whether they are having the desired effect is important. Regularly spaced appointments with the nutritionist will be important until the treatment regime is going smoothly. During these appointments, acknowledgment of successes is motivating. They also provide an opportunity to make any necessary changes. Over time, the treatment regimen will most likely change as goals are met, new factors emerge, insight and knowledge acquired, and new goals are set. It is hoped that treatment will evolve to where it is no longer treatment but is in fact a new way of life.

Fitness Coaching

Mark Jenkins

Point Of View

As a trainer who has worked with a slew of performing artists, I realize how much of an anchor proper exercise and diet can be. I have clients who won't even record unless they are training, much to the record company's dismay! To someone who is dealing with bipolar or depression, the need for such an anchor is even greater.

Having your body fall apart will only make it harder to handle bipolar or depression. It is hard enough to battle your mind. Neglecting your body will only make the battle more difficult to win. Keeping good physical habits will give you an edge. Being in great shape can be the difference between a depression that puts you out of action and one that only slows you down. A recent study[1] suggests that exercising three times a week may be just as effective in relieving the symptoms of major depression as the standard treatment of anti-depressant medications. A conditioned body might help you with the challenges of excess energy and inability to focus that often accompanies mania.

There are four main areas to consider in taking care of your body in addition to good nutrition. Optimal physical

---

1 Blumenthal JA; Babyak MA; Moore KA; Craighead WE; Herman S; Khatri P; Waugh R; Napolitano MA; Forman LM; Appelbaum M; Doraiswamy PM; Krishnan KR. (1999). Effects of exercise training on older patients with major depression. Arch Intern Med, 159:19, 2349-56

fitness is only achieved by combining all four types of exercise with a diet that supports you well. The four types are strength, endurance, flexibility, and body awareness. Strength is best developed with resistive weight training. Endurance is increased via aerobic exercise. Flexibility comes through stretching. Body awareness is achieved through dance, yoga, tai chi, or the many activities that have you focused during movement.

Integration With Team

Fitness coaches are likely to spend more time with the client than any other team member with the exception of family and friends. They see physical changes that other members often miss. Sharing their observations can help the therapists and other team members catch depressions much earlier. They can also help clients to recognize the need for increased attention by the other team members.

The fitness coach motivates clients to get out where they interact with others. One of the negative effects of depression is to isolate from others and lose motivation. The coach can also encourage the client to go outside and get much needed sunshine. Exercise works to help change the negative patterns and leads to greater compliance with the other components of a program.

Assessment Process

Assessments are an important step before taking on any new exercise routine. Knowledge of your current condition can help avoid injury and make sure the program will be one that can be followed. Assessments can be as complex as body composition analysis and VO2 Max testing, or as simple as testing for ability to lift weights and touch your toes. It is important to set the baseline condition as well as periodically test for changes. Periodic assessments can help in analyzing the effectiveness of specific exercises and be used in making changes to the program.

A typical thorough assessment may include:

◇ Health History & Medical Screening
◇ Vital Sign Measurements
◇ Body Composition
◇ Cardiovascular Endurance
◇ Strength and Muscular Endurance
◇ Flexibility Testing

Goal Setting

The expertise of the fitness coach is critical in goal setting. While setting goals that are unreasonable can discourage the client from continuing with the program, goals that are too easy can result in boredom and disillusionment with the idea that making progress is based on effort. This disillusionment can spill over into the other aspects of the integrated program. A good coach knows from experience what goals to set and how hard the client is going to push to achieve them. The coach can also guide the client in adjusting the goals according to current mental conditions that affect motivation.

The advantage of fitness goals is that they are very specific and measurable. You either ran five miles or not; there is no ambiguity about it. The clarity of goals combined with achieving them gives the client self-esteem and faith that the less measurable mental goals can also be accomplished.

Treatment

The best fitness program is one that the client will do. The program needs to be adapted to each individual so as to keep up motivation. This is accomplished by finding the right mix of exercises that address the strength, endurance, flexibility, and body awareness needs while matching the interests of the client.

A unique blend of skill and creativity is what sets the great trainer apart from others. Anyone can change their body type if they can stick with a program, often consisting of an innovative fusion of pilates, calisthenics, sports drills, weight training, and high intensity cardio. The trainer needs to keep the custom-fit workout sessions fresh by incorporating a wide range of sweat-inducing activities, such as boxing, bungee cords, and kettlebells. I never give the same workout session twice. Staying away from routine keeps the muscles and mind constantly stimulated.

Primary Care Physician

Will Meecham, MD

Point Of View

Our brains and bodies are one. The brain directs the activities of the body, while the body provides the environment the brain needs to work properly. Neither can function without the other. As a result, the health of our bodies must not be ignored when we work to improve our mental wellness. There are many ways in which emotional wellness or distress influence somatic health, and vice versa.

For instance, an occasional case of what looks like psychiatric illness is discovered to be due to thyroid dysfunction. The early stages of dementia sometimes manifest as behavioral disturbances. It is important to detect such conditions in order to ensure proper diagnosis and avoid inappropriate treatments.

Chronic pain can exacerbate depression, as well as be worsened by it. Similarly, it is well known that emotional stress and heart disease are interrelated. Immune competence appears to be influenced by emotional states. These bidirectional influences between bodily and mental health are probably the rule rather than the exception, though the strength of the associations vary widely.

At the same time, the qualities of nutrition, rest, and conditioning all influence mental well-being. Although frequently overstated, the "sugar rush" and subsequent "crash" are widely known results of a particular kind of improper nutrition. Alterations in the sleep-wake cycle occur commonly when moods fluctuate in bipolar conditions, while shift work and jet lag have been observed to set off mood crises.

Finally, medications for psychiatric disorders may have substantial medical consequences. Weight gain, neurologic symptoms, and sexual dysfunction are common side effects. At the same time, some drugs for medical conditions alter moods, cause anxiety, disrupt the sleep-wake cycle, etc.

Success in the Bipolar Advantage program therefore requires the participation of medical practitioners. Depending on the client's situation and preference, medical workup and management may be the responsibility of his or her existing primary care provider. Alternatively, members of the Advantage medical staff can take on this role.

Integration With Team

A medical perspective ensures that focus on mental wellness does not become too narrow, and that the health of the body, the brain's companion, is kept in mind. The practitioner brings a biological perspective to the table. In many cases, an initial evaluation provides a "clean bill of health." Afterwards, the client's Advantage team can direct the journey toward *Results Worth Striving For* assured that there are no hidden medical problems which might affect or be affected by its recommendations.

Other times, ongoing or newly discovered medical conditions need to be managed so that the person's comfort level, physical functioning, and longevity are maximized. In these cases, the rest of the team is kept appraised of changes in medication, physical capabilities, recommended nutrition, or needs for any specific therapy. If psychiatric pharmaceuticals are part of the client's program, the medical practitioner works closely with the psychiatrist to ensure that drugs are chosen that carry the least risk to the body's health, are compatible with any other medications the client takes, and that somatic side effects are anticipated and dealt with appropriately.

Assessment Process

The medical assessment is tailored to the client, but emphasizes identification of illnesses known to be common in those with psychiatric disorders. In particular, attention is paid to detecting medical conditions that might cause symptoms of mental illness. In addition, any limitations on exercise capability are identified, so that the regimen of vigorous physical activity that is part of the Advantage Program can be tailored to the client's strengths and limitations.

The medical provider obtains a detailed medical history, keeping in mind the presence of a psychiatric condition. A thorough history documents prior medical disorders, and sometimes unearths symptoms suggestive of illnesses that might explain or result from psychiatric problems, or that necessitate adjustments to the Advantage Program. A thorough physical examination identifies problems that need further assessment. Comprehensive laboratory studies are ordered to identify metabolic, endocrine, hematologic, infectious, inflammatory, neoplastic, and other diseases. An EKG is obtained to help rule out occult cardiac disorders. Diagnostic imaging is arranged as indicated. Most clients benefit from a brain MRI to eliminate concern that structural brain abnormalities might be causing their symptoms.

Additional studies may be required, depending on the client's age and prior history, the results of the physical examination, and initial diagnostic investigations. Some clients require an EEG to further evaluate neurologic and/or psychiatric symptoms. In other cases, sleep studies or exercise stress tests may be indicated. Obviously, the list of possible diagnostic studies is long and depends on findings in each case. The goal, however, is always to maximize the client's general health and his or her ability to safely achieve *Results Worth Striving For.*

Goal Setting

Medical goals in the Advantage Program are similar to those for the general public. However, people with mental illness often have increased sensitivity to bodily imbalances. Therefore, it is of paramount importance that the Advantage client works toward a healthful regimen of nutrition, exercise, and sleep hygiene. Although other team members usually direct the client as lifestyle goals are formulated, the medical provider oversees the plan. He or she also follows the client over time to be sure the lifestyle changes are well tolerated by the body.

The client's medical history at intake and any newly discovered physical disorders dictate whether the medical provider suggests specific additional goals. Whenever possible, attempts are made to bring the body into a state of optimal health with a minimum of medical intervention. For this reason, and in order to further the client's mental wellness, a healthy lifestyle is one of the pillars of the Advantage Program.

Treatment

Other team members help the client achieve the desired changes to diet, exercise, substance use, sleep, and so on. However, the medical provider maintains oversight in order to ensure safety and optimal results with regards to bodily health. Where necessary, the provider prescribes medications and other treatments for physical conditions, whether ongoing or newly discovered in the course of the Advantage medical workup.

Specific behavioral improvements are frequently advised. Smoking cessation aids will be prescribed as needed. Medical assistance with substance abuse recovery is provided when necessary. Dietary changes may be indicated to reduce weight, improve cholesterol profiles, decrease fasting glucose levels, or lower blood pressure. Hopefully, such changes will forestall the need for medication to manage hypercholesterolemia, hypertension, or diabetes.

When needed, the patient may be referred for outside management of complex medical conditions. However, conservative measures are preferred when possible, and the medical provider works with the rest of the team to help optimize the client's bodily health, comfort, and longevity. The medical perspective ensures that *Results Worth Striving For*

include improvement in bodily health as well as mental
well-being.

Where Do We Go From Here?

"The problem is not that we are mentally ill; the problem is that we experience 150 percent of what 'normal' people do and we are frustrated that we have not yet learned how to handle it."
- *The Depression Advantage*[1]

After writing this book for several months while in a very deep depression, I find myself in a mania triggered by the excitement of nearing completion. Enjoying the grandiosity, I find myself contemplating what the world will be like when enough people share the perspective of *Bipolar In Order*.

Imagine if The Juilliard School had the insight to recognize Nathaniel Ayers' condition before he lost control, and the wisdom to match him with a peer that had the condition "in order." Steve Lopez would have had to use his genius on another subject, and the world would be deprived of a masterpiece of both writing[2] and cinema,[3] but what could Nathaniel have become?

---

1 Wootton, Tom, The Depression Advantage, 2007 Bipolar Advantage Publishers, CA

2 Lopez, Steve, The Soloist, 2008, Berkley Books by Penguin, NY

3 Grant, Susannah, Screenplay based on the book by Steve Lopez, The Soloist Movie, 2009, Dreamworks and Universal Pictures

It is not too late for Nathaniel or many others that were left behind by the culture of low expectations in current recovery models. Now we can see depression, mania, hallucination, and delusion from a different perspective. What of the millions of people who's diagnosis can be the beginning of a life of greatness? Instead of having to unlearn negative beliefs and fears that are deeply imbedded in the current paradigm of mental illness, they could begin on a path to understanding and power over their conditions right away.

It will take time to create this paradigm shift, but it has already begun. The ideas in this book seem radical, but from my perspective they are so obvious that it is only a matter of persuading more people to try. We are actually a lot further along than one might think. It is encouraging that mental health professionals, therapists, and families everywhere have found the goals presented here and in my talks to be logical and attainable.

Thousands of people have already accepted the value of Insight, Freedom, Stability, Self-Mastery, and Equanimity. Many have contacted us with their stories of success on the path to *Bipolar In Order*. What we need most is for you to make the effort to get your own life "in order." Whether you have a mental condition, or are a therapist, psychiatrist, or family member, changing the status quo in mental health is a goal worth striving for.

About The Contributors

Peter Forster, MD

Dr. Peter Forster is a Clinical Professor of Psychiatry at the University of California, San Francisco; an editor of "Emergency Psychiatry," the publication of the American Association for Emergency Psychiatry; past president of the Northern California Psychiatric Society; and a Distinguished Fellow of the American Psychiatric Association.

Dr. Forster specializes in the assessment of the standard of care in suicidal and crisis patients. An internationally respected expert, he has written many articles on psychiatric emergencies, mood disorders, anxiety, somatization, and managed care.

In his private practice, www.gatewaypsychiatric.com, Dr. Forster specializes in the evaluation and treatment of adult depression, bipolar disorder (manic-depression), anxiety, panic disorders, phobias, and stress reactions.

"I believe that caring and respectful relationships are the basis for any kind of healing. In my work with patients I view what we do together as a collaboration. You are the expert in yourself and your feelings, I bring to that collaboration the expertise from my academic experience and training as well as from the care of thousands of patients with similar problems. Together we create a treatment plan that will lead to a sustained recovery from a mood or anxiety disorder."

Rochelle I. Frank, PhD

Shelly Frank received her PhD in Clinical Psychology from Syracuse University, and completed her clinical training at the Yale Psychiatric Institute. She specializes in evidence-based treatment of clinically complex emotional and behavioral disorders in adolescents and adults, and also has expertise with couples and families. Dr. Frank completed post-graduate training programs in dialectical behavior therapy, prolonged exposure therapy, and cognitive behavioral analysis system of psychotherapy. She has over 20 years of experience across treatment settings.

Dr. Frank was a supervising psychologist within the New York State Department of Mental Health, and in San Francisco was the chief psychologist for a residential treatment program before becoming the clinical director of Family Mosaic Project, during which time she served on numerous policy and programming committees within the Behavioral Health Services division of the Department of Public Health. In addition to her private practice in Oakland, CA, Shelly conducts clinical research on self-monitoring and emotion regulation, and is on staff at Gateway Psychiatric Services.

Dr. Frank is an assistant clinical professor in the Clinical Sciences Training Program at U.C. Berkeley, and in the Department of Psychiatry at U.C.S.F. School of Medicine. Shelly also is an adjunct professor of clinical psychology at Argosy University and a clinical supervisor at The Wright Institute, and currently is the 2009 President of the Alameda County Psychological Association.

www.DrRochelleFrank.com

Maureen Duffy, PhD

Maureen Duffy is a professor of counseling and family therapy and a practicing couples and family therapist. She is highly regarded in the marriage and family therapy world and is on the editorial boards of The Journal of Marital and Family Therapy, The Family Journal, and The Journal of Systemic Therapies. She is the Co-Editor of The Qualitative Report, a journal dedicated to qualitative research. She is also the Co-Editor of the "Family and Health" column in The Family Journal. She has presented her work at major professional conferences nationally and internationally. In 2006, Maureen was an invited speaker at the Oxford University Round Table on the Psychology of the Child. She is the author of numerous publications in family therapy and qualitative research.

Maureen is fascinated by how the brain is shaped by what we think and do and by how often we think and do it. She takes very seriously the fact that the brain changes throughout life and that the direction of those changes is influenced by the quality of our relationships, our behaviors, and our thoughts and feelings. Maureen is personally and professionally committed to breaking the link between the diagnosis of a mental illness and the taking on of the traditional identity of a mentally ill person. She believes that mood disorders like bipolar and major depression are brain disorders, not personal identities, and not primary careers. Her work also extends, with humor and compassion, to the parents and friends and families of those diagnosed with mood disorders.

Brian Weller

Brian is the creator and presenter for the Bipolar Advantage Mind Skills Workshops. Since the early 1970's, he has brought meditation to thousands of people across the world. He is a management training development expert to many international corporations including Shell International Petroleum, IBM, and Imperial Chemical Industries, and has founded 2 businesses specializing in learning skills. His work with the British Civil Service during the 1980's in organizational transformation seminars and stress management workshops were widely acclaimed.

Brian is one of the founders of the economic localization and sustainability movement and runs seminars for community leaders in the US and Europe who are preparing for peak oil and climate change. His passion for Mind Skills began in the late 1970's. As one of the originators of mind-mapping, his advanced memory, creativity, and personal change training has inspired thousands of people in business and public settings to reach their full potential. He is also a strategic advisor to some internet start up companies in California who are creating the next generation of software for the emerging 3.0 semantic web.

Scott Sullender, PhD

Scott is an ordained Presbyterian minister, a licensed Psychologist (PSY 8931) and a Diplomate with the American Association of Pastoral Counselors. He has over 35 years of professional experience as a pastor, pastoral counselor, non-profit organizational executive, psychologist, and author/writer. He has made a specialty of providing psychological assessments and various kinds of self-improvement workshops for Protestant ministers and seminarians.

Scott is currently employed as Associate Professor of Pastoral Counseling at San Francisco Theological Seminary, San Anselmo and Pasadena California. He is the primary instructor in the seminary's Doctor of Ministry in Pastoral Care and Counseling program. His teaching load includes classes in Counseling and Psychotherapy, Psychology of Religion, Spirituality and Spiritual Direction, Abnormal Psychology and Diagnosis, Loss and Bereavement, Addictions Counseling, and Psychology of Aging and Adult Development.

In addition to his teaching duties, he is a practicing pastoral psychotherapist. He specializes in the integration of spirituality and psychotherapy.

He is the author of several books and scholarly articles. His books include, *Losses in Later Life: A new way of walking with God* and *Grief and Growth: Pastoral Resources for Emotional & Spiritual Growth.*

James W. Jordan, Jr.

Mr. Jordan is the Executive Director for NAMI Pennsylvania. He has been Executive Assistant to the Governor of Michigan; a Deputy Secretary in the Pennsylvania Department of Health; and a Vice President in North Broward Hospital District. He has served as the Director for the Department of Health and Rehabilitation and the Department of Health and Public Safety in Essex County, New Jersey and Broward County, Florida.

During the past twenty years he has managed a 1,200-bed psychiatric hospital and a 330 bed geriatric center. He has managed a drug treatment program; 110 bed psychiatric treatment and rehabilitation program; and a sexual assault treatment program. Mr. Jordan established and operated industrial and occupational medicine programs and established two adult level 2 trauma centers and one pediatric trauma center. He designed and managed numerous health care programs ranging from trauma systems to primary care and community programs.

Mr. Jordan established the Michigan Refugee Relief Fund, which raised funds to purchase food, medical supplies, and medical personnel.

Mr. Jordan holds a master's degree in clinical psychology and participated in the Senior Management Program for State and Local Government at the Kennedy School of Government at Harvard University. In addition, a scholarship at Nova University was named for Mr. Jordan in recognition of his contributions to health care.

Michael R. Edelstein, PhD

Dr. Edelstein has an in-person and telephone therapy practice in San Francisco. He is the author of *Three Minute Therapy*,[1] a self-help book for overcoming common emotional and behavioral problems, for which he has been awarded Author of the Year.

In his practice, Dr. Edelstein specializes in the treatment of anxiety, depression, relationship problems, and addictions. He is also the San Francisco SMART Recovery Professional Advisor.

Dr. Edelstein was a Training Supervisor and Fellow of the Albert Ellis Institute. He is Past President of the Association for Behavioral and Cognitive Therapy.

REBT/CBT is a modern approach to overcoming emotional and behavioral disturbance. It focuses on the present and helps clients take an active role in their recovery. It helps clients identify the unrealistic beliefs at the core of their psychological problems and gives them powerful tools they can use to change their thinking and dramatically improve their lives.

www.ThreeMinuteTherapy.com

---

[1] Edelstein, Dr. Michael R., Three Minute Therapy, 1997, Glenbridge Publishing, Colorado
www.threeminutetherapy.com

Maria Chang-Calderon, PhD(c), MSHR

Maria is a doctoral candidate at Alliant International University, Marshall Goldsmith School of Management in the field of Organizational Psychology. She has been a Human Resources professional for more than 10 years, specializing in staffing and, most recently, career management counseling for persons with bipolar disorder.

Maria provides an array of career counseling services for management professionals who have bipolar disorder and who are interested in maintaining their competitive edge, as well as those interested in joining the management ranks of major organizations.

She offers professional career management counseling for all persons with bipolar disorder. Maria's counseling services focus on helping individuals build on their strengths in relation to their workplace conditions. These services do not include jobseeker employment placements. This type of career management counseling is aimed at increasing an individual's knowledge, skills, and abilities based on a comprehensive talent assessment, performance coaching, and strategic career development planning.

Maria's research interests include topics such as organization empowerment, inclusion, and social responsibility. She is committed to enabling the success of individuals who have bipolar disorder in professional or management roles within major organizations.

Denise K. Hughes, MA

Denise Hughes is a writer, speaker and Financial Coach/Consultant. She has a strong national presence in the financial community.

She has been quoted numerous times in The Wall Street Journal "Love and Money" column, and is a major contributor to The Wall Street Journalist, Jeff Opdyke's Book, *Love and Money*. Denise has also been noted in the Journal of Financial Planning, Reader's Digest, California Woman and Parenting Magazine. Denise writes her own monthly finance column for the ezine www.50fabulous.com.

She has presented at regional and national financial planning conferences. In 2008, she was sponsored by AIG for the national organization "Make Mine a Million." She coached business women across America in taking their businesses to the million dollar mark.

Her mission is to educate, empower, and enlighten her clients in order for them to reach their full financial potential. She does this by breaking through limiting money mind-sets and behavior patterns and supporting clients in practicing financially mature behaviors.

www.denisehughes.org

Justin Liu, MD

Dr. Justin Liu completed his undergraduate premedical training at the University of California at Berkeley, graduating with honors. Dr. Liu received his Medical Degree from Loma Linda University School of Medicine and completed his residency in Physical Medicine & Rehabilitation at Stanford University. Dr. Liu is Board-Certified by the American Board of Physical Medicine & Rehabilitation. For 5 years, Dr. Liu served as the Chair of Back & Trauma Rehabilitation for St. Mary's Medical Center in San Francisco, California. During that time, he played an active role as a Clinical Professor for the Stanford University Physical Medicine & Rehabilitation Residency Program.

Dr. Liu currently serves as the Medical Director of Physical Medicine & Rehabilitation at John Muir Medical Center in Walnut Creek, California. In both the inpatient and outpatient settings, Dr. Liu coordinates a multidisciplinary team of rehabilitation therapists, physicians, nurses, and neuropsychologists to help create therapy programs custom-tailored to each patient's individual needs.

As featured by CNBC, CNET, KTVU-2, KRON-4, AsianWeek, FLYP Media, and Ebony Magazine, Dr. Liu has successfully implemented use of the Nintendo Wii to help treat patients who have sustained various neurological injuries. Dr. Liu continuously strives to further develop the field of "Wii-Hab."

www.WiiHabMedicine.com

Ruth Leyse-Wallace PhD, RD

Dr. Leyse-Wallace has practiced clinical dietetics in psychiatric hospitals, treatment programs, outpatient clinics, and in private practice for more than twenty-five years.

Her clinical experience includes practice at The Menninger Foundation (Topeka, Kansas), Sharp Mesa Vista Hospital (San Diego, California), Sierra Tucson (Tucson, Arizona), HCA Willow Park Hospital (Plano, Texas) and Osawatomie State Hospital (Osawatomie, Kansas).

In addition to her interest in mental health and the PsychoNutriologic Person, her special areas of clinical interest include the nutrition-focused physical examination, eating disorders, and alcoholism.

Her professional activities also include writing (*Linking Nutrition to Mental Health: A Scientific Exploration* and *The Metaparadigm of Clinical Dietetics: Derivation and Applications*) and producing educational materials as well as lectures and workshops for professional and public audiences. She served as an adjunct faculty member at Mesa College in San Diego, California.

Ruth's education includes a PhD from the University of Arizona in 1998, a dietetic internship with a master's degree from the University of Kansas, and graduation with Phi Kappa Phi honors and a B.S. degree from the University of California at Davis. Dr. Leyse-Wallace now lives in Alpine, California. Her website is at www.RuthLeyseWallace.com

Mark Jenkins

When it comes to perfecting body image, Mark Jenkins sets the standard for not only looking good, but feeling good as well. The highly recruited fitness trainer and motivator has worked with an array of prominent figures including Bad Boy CEO (Sean "Diddy" Combs), business executives (Benny Medina, Chris Lighty & Andre Harrell), former Essence director (Susan Taylor), famed lawyer (Johnny Cochran), director (Tyler Perry), radio personality (Angie Martinez) and A-list entertainers (Mary J. Blige, Beyonce', Busta Rhymes, L.L. Cool J, Eve, Q-Tip, Anthony Hamilton, N.O.R.E, Missy Elliott, Brandy, D'Angelo).

Through the lifestyle brand InFitness, the unorthodox health guru is determined to assist people with becoming their phenomenal best. His book, *Jump Off: 60 Days to a Hip Hop Hard Body* (Harper Collins), is an inspiring success story about the benefits of discipline, following one's dreams, and opening up people's minds to look at exercise as a habit as natural as breathing.

In addition to his personal training schedule, Jenkins also has his hands full in various facets of the fitness business. He developed his own supplement line available at MJE3.com in 2009. He has lent his expertise to various networks including BET, VH-1 and MTV as well as shows such as Fit TV, E! Entertainment, EXTRA, and recently appearing alongside Mary J. Blige on The Tyra Banks Show. Mark is spokesperson for the United Ways Fun Fly & Fit program.

Will Meecham, MD

Will Meecham, MD, MA, studied neuronal electro-physiology as a Biophysics graduate student. After medical school, he trained as an ophthalmologist, and then specialized in ocular oncology and ophthalmic plastic and reconstructive surgery. He has published articles about ocular malignancies, eyelid reconstruction, and radiation biology. Until medical issues forced early retirement from surgical work, Dr. Meecham practiced as an oculoplastic surgeon and periocular oncologist at Kaiser Permanente.

In exploring new career paths, he forayed into computer programming and biomedical informatics. He also worked at the California Department of Public Health, instructing physician audiences throughout the state about the neurologic and other effects of childhood lead poisoning.

As a psychiatry client with a bipolar diagnosis, he has spent many years developing his own approach to mental conditions, which he views from both biological and spiritual perspectives. He currently contributes regularly to his online journal at WillSpirit.com, discussing topics such as the physiology of psychiatric medications, behavioral approaches to mood management, current societal attitudes toward people with psychiatric issues, and the biological foundations of spirituality.

Active in the mental health community in Marin County, California, he works in the local Suicide Prevention program and also provides services as a Patient's Rights Advocate.

About The Author

Tom Wootton founded Bipolar Advantage with the mission to help people with mental conditions shift their thinking and behavior so that they can lead extraordinary lives. He challenges many of the pervasive attitudes about mental conditions and charts a different course that looks at the positive as well as negative aspects of mental conditions. He has worked tirelessly to change the paradigm of how we look at and treat mental conditions.

Tom specialized in advanced, accelerative learning systems, which he taught to corporations, colleges, and high schools. His clients included: Visa, HP, Cisco, Ford, British Telecom, NSA, AT&T, Charles Schwab, Nokia, and many more worldwide. He began teaching workshops that he designed for bipolar and depression in 2002.

Tom Wootton has become a widely recognized speaker nationwide as a passionate agent of change in the field of mental health. He has given lectures and workshops for mental health advocacy groups, doctors, professionals, family and friends, and, of course, those who have mental conditions. Mental health clients include Kaiser Permanente, Orange County Behavioral Health, Riverside County Behavioral Health, San Bernardino County Behavioral Health, Mental Health Associations throughout California, and NAMI organizations nationwide.

Other books by the author are *The Bipolar Advantage*(2005) and *The Depression Advantage*(2007).

CPSIA information can be obtained at www.ICGtesting.com
Printed in the USA
BVOW012136290412

288897BV00002B/3/P